THE AUTHOR

Cecil Northcott is a graduate of Cambridge University and a Congregational minister. For fifteen years he was one of the secretaries of the London Missionary Society, which first awoke his interest in Africa, and he was later General Secretary of the United Council for Missionary Education at Edinburgh House. He has visited Africa on a number of occasions during the last ten years, traveling over the Moffat routes in South Africa, Bechuanaland, and Southern Rhodesia. In 1961 he lectured in twenty liberal arts colleges in the United States on Africa on behalf of the Association of American Colleges. Dr. Northcott is Editorial Secretary of the Lutterworth Press, London. He is the author of a definitive biography of Robert Moffat and of *Hymns We Love* (see back of jacket).

CHRISTIANITY IN AFRICA

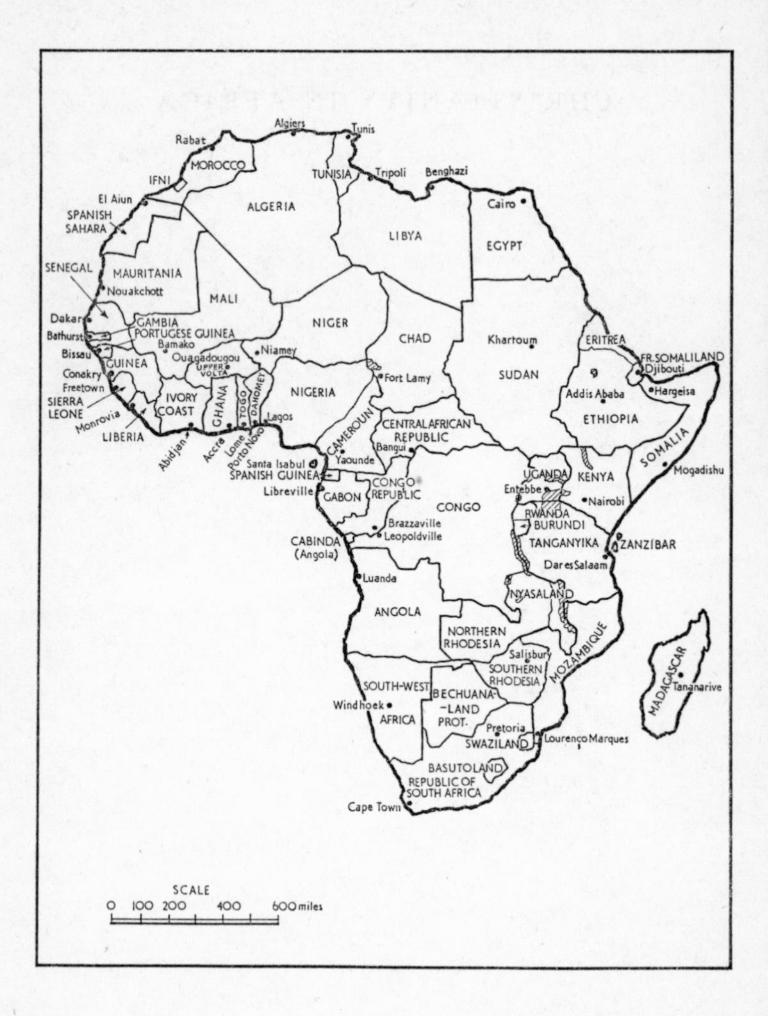

Algiers
Tunis
Rabat
MOROCCO
IFNI
TUNISIA
Tripoli
Benghazi
El Aiun
SPANISH
SAHARA
ALGERIA
Cairo
LIBYA
EGYPT
SENEGAL
MAURITANIA
Nouakchott
MALI
Dakar
GAMBIA
Bathurst
PORTUGESE GUINEA
Bamako
NIGER
CHAD
Khartoum
ERITREA
FR. SOMALILAND
Djibouti
Bissau
GUINEA
Ouagadougou
Niamey
UPPER VOLTA
Conakry
Freetown
SIERRA
LEONE
Monrovia
LIBERIA
IVORY
COAST
GHANA
TOGO
DAHOMEY
NIGERIA
Fort Lamy
SUDAN
Addis Ababa
Hargeisa
ETHIOPIA
Lagos
Abidjan
Accra
Lome
Porto Novo
CAMEROUN
Yaounde
CENTRAL AFRICAN
REPUBLIC
Bangui
SOMALIA
Mogadishu
Santa Isabul
SPANISH GUINEA
UGANDA
KENYA
Entebbe
Nairobi
Libreville
GABON
CONGO
REPUBLIC
CONGO
RWANDA
BURUNDI
Brazzaville
Leopoldville
CABINDA
(Angola)
TANGANYIKA
ZANZIBAR
Dar es Salaam
Luanda
NYASALAND
ANGOLA
NORTHERN
RHODESIA
MOZAMBIQUE
Salisbury
SOUTHERN
RHODESIA
MADAGASCAR
Tananarive
SOUTH-WEST
AFRICA
Windhoek
BECHUANA-
-LAND
PROT.
Pretoria
SWAZILAND
Lourenço Marques
BASUTOLAND
REPUBLIC OF
SOUTH AFRICA
Cape Town
SCALE
0 100 200 400 600 miles

CHRISTIANITY IN AFRICA

CECIL NORTHCOTT

*

Philadelphia
The Westminster Press

FIRST PUBLISHED 1963

PRINTED IN GREAT BRITAIN

CONTENTS

PREFACE

THIS little book is offered rather rashly as a passing commentary on the African Christian scene, and obviously, amidst all the voluminous literature now pouring out on Africa, has very severe limitations. In any case it will be out of date, as it ought to be, before long. But I hope that some of the things said in it have an abiding value for the observer of Africa, this continent that is going to keep the world on tenterhooks for the next century even as it fascinated the century that is past.

Christianity is in a tight spot in Africa: some would say a very tight spot. It is therefore all-important that Christians should understand something of its position, which cannot be done without trying to understand a lot of other things. That is why I have had to pack so much into so little and I readily agree with the critics who may point this out. There are always perils in dealing with Africa and one of them is making judgments from a little knowledge. I hope I have avoided those judgments.

If I had to name four books for the reader who wants to get a little deeper into the 'soul of Africa' I think they would be Bengt Sundkler's *The Christian Ministry in Africa*, F. W. Welbourn's *East African Rebels* (both SCM Press), Sundkler's *Bantu Prophets in South Africa* (2nd edition, Oxford University Press for Institute of African Affairs) and Mia Brandel-Syrier's *Black Woman in Search of God* (Lutterworth Press). In the last chapter of this book I have used some illustrations which were previously included, rather differently, in a group of BBC talks and then published as *Good News from Africa* (Independent Press).

C.N.

1

EVERY MAN HIS OWN AFRICA

MY AFRICA is the thunder of the rain on the tin roofs of Freetown and the surprise that everything was so green when I had expected, from the imagined image of Africa, dun brown acres of sand and barren soil. From Dakar down the west coast, the panorama underneath the wings of the aeroplane lay as a tufted green expanse of little trees, bee-hive huts and twisted lagoons. Over there, beyond the hazy horizon, was more Africa, on and on for thousands of miles until you reached the Indian Ocean. Africa is the continent between the great seas, and here on the Atlantic rim the rain drummed down.

Africa is also the line of jacaranda-purple trees on Delamere Avenue, Nairobi, and Jameson Avenue, Salisbury: cities of the settler or Africa's white burden according to the view you take of the white man's excursion into this black man's continent. In cities like Casablanca, the gleam of reinforced concrete; in Lagos, the magnificence of the Federal Palace Hotel built on a raft of the same stuff; in Johannesburg, the vulgar excrescences of skyscrapers lapped with gold; in Accra the flashy wonder of the Nkrumah party's headquarters, and the elegant, erudite campus of the University on Legon Hill.

Africa for me is always a rose in December on the high plateau of Jos in Nigeria. The mornings dawn in cool splendour, and the sun at high noon is bearable enough to walk. The English rose, some white man's nostalgia for home, flourished in a kind of gay nonchalance against the harsh, bleak expanse of the Jos terrain.

I remembered it as I sat in a little mud church out on the plateau where a handful of Birom people gathered for the holy mysteries. The benches were hard baked mud, and so was the Holy Table where a tattered Bible rested in eternal dust as the African minister (hotly dog collared) led the responses. It was cold under the thatched roof, with shafts of sharp sunlight shooting through the gaps of the thatch throwing a bespattered pattern over the bowed group. They were magnificently black in the majestic style of these parts, and all about the little church was the farm, corn, smell of the tall grass stockades where the people lived.

The smells of Africa linger in the nostrils. The smell of dust, the ever-present floating curtain of sunlit haze redolent with the smell of cattle, manure of beast and human. Dust envelops the dirt roads of the Rhodesias as the station wagons and the Cape-to-Cairo buses plunge down the high road into Tanganyika and on into Kenya. You pull on to the soft shoulder of the road, and show your Christian forbearance by slowing down to make less dust for the other man, a sort of African Samaritanism more observed in omission than commission.

Africa is the smell of the evening meal in a bush village, as the crackle of the wood fire underneath the pot throws sparks into the dimming light, and the women call the children and the children call everybody. It is the smell of one of those great West African markets. It could be Kano, or Kumasi, or that fantastic covered one at Onitsha on the Niger where everything from Germany to Japan is for sale, and the heaving mass of buyers and sellers create an entrenched market perfume.

The eye, too, is for Africa. For me it scans an impeccably blue morning on the edges of the Kalahari Desert in Bechuanaland when the red earth, the unfaltering sky and the golden blaze of the sun wove the authentic African image of heat. It was hot, not the lazy buttercup heat of an English

June but the furnace fire of the December sun when the cattle pant for the thin shade of a thorn tree and the humans reach for the drinks.

An empty land this? I walked away from the lorry I was in to see and feel the silence of Africa as the hot earth smote the feet. All round me were the huge protuberances and defiles of the Lithubaruba Hills where the Bechuana Chief Sechele sheltered from the attacking Boers, and where a group of German missionaries in the middle of the last century wrestled for his soul. I found the granite cross that marks their graves, 'Schroeder, Herbst, Backeberg and two children', in the deep silence of the bush. At once the bush was filled with the spirits of Africa's past, the solemn men and women who trudged this road, egging on the unwilling oxen, preaching their good news in unfamiliar tongues and then dying of fever and heat.

Africa looks empty to the unpractised eye. But the continent has an uncanny way of coming alive either through the eye of memory or in present happenings. I had left the mission doctor bending over the engine of his lorry as men often do in Africa, cursing or caressing. The contraption had just jolted to a stop: it was plainly too hot to go on. But the dispensary and the patients were waiting, and the doctor was a dedicated man who knew his Africa. He too sat in the shade of the lorry waiting for Africa to come to the rescue.

One by one along the track rattled an African truck driver and an Indian trader from Johannesburg, accompanied by a host of attendant laughing crews who enjoyed the doctor's predicament. They pulled and shoved and encouraged the lorry, as you would an old and tired horse, with tremendous cheers which at last proved effective. No one could stay for polite thanks, in case all the engines failed.

This road, I remembered, was once the main road from south to north. It ran from Robert Moffat's frontier mission station at Kuruman (now in the Northern Cape) to the Zambesi, where on the outer rim of Victorian Africa, David Livingstone threshed about in a mixture of exploration and Christian dreams. This was the 'missionaries' road, a free life-line of comings and goings. It kept open the way to the north against aggression of Boers and Bantu alike, one of the many Christian roads in Africa that struck into the interior long before the colonial scramble for Central Africa was thought of. Other roads ran inland from Zanzibar to the great lakes; from Lagos to the boundaries of the Sahara. They carried a strange assortment of men and women from Boston and the Rhineland, from Glasgow and London, under the impulse of the Christian gospel, and the milestones along the roads today are chiefly the graves of those who died on the march.

It requires the eye of faith to see what these expeditions of simple valour and dedication accomplished in Africa, for so much of the Christian investment in Africa has been lost in the jungle of vegetation and events. Even the greatest of those who in the last century illumined the tracks of Africa with their own daring and death, David Livingstone, left a glowing name, but as a missionary very little else.

I turned off the 'missionaries' road' to see Livingstone's home at Kolobeng in a pocket of hills, silent and remote where the Kolobeng stream rushes in a bright torrent in time of rain. There is the mound of his little £25 house, overgrown, lit with the glistening yellow of the mimosa of which I plucked a blossom for keepsake. There is the grave of his infant daughter Elizabeth, lonely in the bush, and over all an air of desertion and decay. Livingstone's heart was away to the horizon and soon his body was there too. He was no settled missionary. For him Africa was a continent of action, and he, the actor and playwright on his self-chosen stage. He mastered a continent but others did the patient planting of the faith.

Africa demands and absorbs all sorts and conditions of

men, and the white man's saga in Africa is a story of occasional conquests but more often of Africa's consuming triumph. It is a continent that kicks back more powerfully than most in size, in climate and in conditions of life. The jungle is ever on the move, the grass is always growing; and the man with the *machette* ever cutting, ever scything —a memorable symbol of the whole continent. Africa drags. She drags at the body and drags at the mind, and the white man falls under the spell of her insidious insistent lethargy. So does the black man. Africa is master of both. She dominates all within her borders.

From these evocative pictures let us turn to some hard facts about this continent that broods over the twentieth century and may be the master continent of the twenty-first.

On the map Africa looks like a question mark, but it is really an exclamation mark set betwixt the New World of the Americas and the Old World of Asia. She counts eleven million square miles against the United States' three and a half million. It is one-fifth of the total land surface of the whole world. Africa could take in the whole of Western Europe and North America, and still have space for most of China.

She is best thought of in regions: the North or Mediterranean Coast, the Sahara Lands, the West Coast, the East Coast, the Central Area, the South Central Area and then the South. These regions are worlds to themselves, but growingly aware that they also are African. Along the North Coast, for instance, the Moroccans, Tunisians, Algerians, Libyans and Egyptians are of the Arab world once securely phalanxed from the rest of Africa by the impenetrable Sahara Desert. But the Sahara is now a bridge rather than a barrier. It links the north with the Africa south of the desert by bus routes, air lines, oil wells and the insistent call of Cairo Radio which invisibly pervades the continent. The East Coast and the West Coast are no longer in remote loneliness from each other: there is a traffic of people, as well as the all-powerful traffic of ideas which spring from such a prophet as Nkrumah of Ghana and his call to the whole continent to think of itself as Africa for the African.

That same note penetrates down through the plateaux of Central and Southern Africa, for it whispers of pan-Africanism, the call of black to black, the overtone of independence and nationhood. This is the hum of a whole continent discovering itself, but still restlessly poised between two worlds and not sure which way to turn. A young Nigerian poet, Mabel Imoukhuede, puts it this way:

Here we stand
infants overblown,
poised between two civilizations,
finding the balance irksome,
itching for something to happen,
to tip us one way or the other,
groping in the dark for a helping hand—
and finding none.
I'm tired, O my God, I'm tired,
I's tired of hanging in the middle way—
But where can I go?[1]

As the colonial map of Africa fades away and the lines drawn by Europe on the face of the land disappear, so these regions of Africa loom into importance as the forerunners of what in the twenty-first century may be the United States of Africa. Geography, climate, distance and separation, which have been Africa's liabilities, are swiftly becoming Africa's assets as the people of the Guinea Gulf discover their brethren on the seaboard of the Indian Ocean and the veld of southern Africa. That which makes an African is not simply a certain pigmentation of the skin but a sense of

[1] Quoted in *Christianity and Crisis*, New York, 20.3.61.

belonging to a particular part of the continent which is at once his and at the same time every African's. What is Africa for Nigeria is also for Nyasaland. The hum of nationalism is also the hum of African inter-nationalism, the rhythm of knowing that you belong to the whole continent even though you may never get beyond the rim of your region. Asked by some Quaker visitors whether he was a Kikuyu or a Kenyan, Jomo Kenyatta replied, 'No, I am an African'.

There are the rivers of Africa. The Nile, the ancient cradle of the world's civilization, bursts out of the high plateau of Uganda and wanders for 4,000 miles through the sands of the Sudan and Egypt. Water is always precious in Africa, and her rivers are personalities—Congo, Niger, Zambesi—clothed with their own life and to be respected as much as people. No one who has stood on the lip of the Victoria Falls and peered into that chasm of foaming water, and watched the rainbows forming and reforming in the sunlit spray of the river, could doubt that the Zambesi is a person of incalculable power. Once the last frontier in the so-called 'dark continent', it now supplies light and power for an immense area of Central Africa, and the dramatic wonder of the falls itself draws the world to see it. Like the Grand Canyon in the United States, the Victoria Falls has never been 'over written': it communicates itself.

I have never climbed a mountain in Africa. But there they are, snow capped, ice cragged, a glimpse of glory from the hot plains—Kilimanjaro, Mount Kenya, Ruwenzori in the east and Mount Cameroon in the west, and Table Mountain at the southern tip. Large parts of Africa are over 3,000 feet, and the central plateaux of the Rhodesias rise to 5,000 feet—a geographical fact which often accounts for short tempers amongst the whites living there, and makes the brittle atmosphere, created by sun and wind, a testy one to live with.

Land and the shape of it create character in Africa. The

Ibo man of Eastern Nigeria, ensconced in his vast village in the rain forest with ample food and a tightly organized community life, is an energetic, confident person compared with, say, the Tonga people of the Zambesi valley, where life is harsh and farming a struggle with a thin soil. The Hausa man of Northern Nigeria, accustomed to the open semi-desert terrain of his country, has perhaps a more resilient independent nature than the domestic Bechuana of southern Africa in the organized wards of their towns and villages.

Land is life in Africa, and the amount of it and the use of it help to stamp the character and customs of the people. Land is the universal link. It speaks for the past of the tribe, the family ancestors and the living hopes of the present and the future. Most of the troubles in Africa between blacks and whites stem from a misunderstanding of the place of land in the life of the people. The most violent of them, the Mau Mau in Kenya, was essentially an eruption caused by the clash of Westernism and tribalism born within the 'land-heart' of the Kikuyu people.

Everybody who thinks of Africa thinks of tribes: the word suggests to the white man a host of black men gathered round the chief either for a consultation or a ceremony. In the Western world we have inherited 'images' of African tribes from travellers' descriptions, from missionaries' reports which suggest that 'tribalism' is a system of the dark ages that must rapidly pass away in modern Africa, and indeed ought to pass away. Leaders of modern Africa gird against tribalism as a hang-over of past days which makes for disunity in a day when the African nations must be united and centrally strong. But 'land' and 'tribe' are still living realities in Africa.

Mr Peter Abrahams, the African writer, says:

> The most important single characteristic of the tribal man is that he is not an individual in the Western sense. Psychologically and emotionally he is the present living

> personification of a number of forces, among the most important of which are the ancestral dead. . . . This society is exclusive and not, like Western society, inclusive . . . anybody not an 'insider' is an enemy, someone to distrust, someone to fear, someone to keep at bay. . . . If you are not in the tribe, there is no way into it. If you are in there is no way out of it except death. Dissent is not recognized. To break the rules of the tribe is to court death.[1]

At the heart of the tribal allegiance is the African eagerness for security. The tribe gives it to him, but under modern pressures the tribal system is disintegrating. Where does he now find security, both physically and psychically? Out of the impetus to answer this question comes the revulsion against the white man and his ways which leads him, in despair, to go back to some of the neglected, disregarded and discredited spirits of his ancestral past as he did in Mau Mau. Below the surface of things in Africa, and penetrating into all aspects of its life, is this search for new roots, new land to plant with ideas and aspirations; the eagerness to have an equivalent in the modern Africa to old Africa's tribal system, which gave a man his abiding place in society and taught him the manners and the methods of ordered living.

It is easy enough to say that Africa is in ferment, and that the ferment is nationalism. This is true, but Africa (contradictory enough) is also quiescent and passive. The tribe, the farm, the garden, the seasons, the customs, conditioned by the rains and the droughts, are still moving in their traditional pattern only faintly disturbed in certain areas, although violently torn in others. In spite of the drift to the urban areas and towns Africa is still predominantly a rural land with populations scattered very unevenly over immense areas.

[1] Quoted in *An African Treasury*, ed. Hughes (Gollancz, 1961), p. 54.

You see this scattered unevenness as you move from one African country to another, from the emptiness of Bechuanaland, where there is only one person to every square mile, to the comparatively crowded Nigeria with over 130 to every square mile. And this sense of a people scattered over the land is supported by the United Nations Report on Economic Development in Africa which showed that Africa's peoples are still mainly country people. In the area south of the Sahara only six millions out of over 230 millions live in towns of twenty thousand or more—a useful figure to remember when the pictures show the seething city crowds.

We see what the crowded towns can do in the Republic of South Africa, where it is now estimated that 35 per cent of the African population (or 3½ millions) is in the urban areas. We see what nation-making means in Ghana or Nigeria. The whole continent in various depths shares the same revolutionary experiences, but the differences in depth are important.

Every man has his own Africa. There are so many of them. Africa has no unity in language, religion, law or custom which help to give cohesion and nationhood to other areas of the world. It is diverse, poor and illiterate in spite of pockets of wealth such as the cocoa and palm oil areas of West Africa, the coffee lands of the East, the copper, gold, diamond and cattle areas of the south-central and south. You drive through the low bush-scrub of Northern Rhodesia and feel the emptiness of the land. Or you walk through Oyo market in Western Nigeria when, at dusk, the minute paraffin lights of a thousand traders scatter a twinkling glow, and you realize how crowded Africa can be.

It is depressing but true to know that a century of contact with the educated white man still leaves Africa practically 50 per cent illiterate amongst its adult population, with illiteracy rates varying from 95 to 99 per cent in

Eritrea to 45 to 50 per cent in Basutoland. It is humiliating to look at a map showing how dominated Africa still is by the carriers of malaria, and to see the massive belt of the continent from coast to coast, and from the southern border of the Sahara to the Limpopo River, marked as endemic for yellow fever and filariasis. The maps showing the areas where leprosy affects ten or more per thousand people, and those where sleeping sickness occurs, are also indications of how prone Africa still is to its primitive scourges.

The United Nations review of economic conditions in Africa (1951) came to the conclusion that 'Africa as a whole is economically among the least developed areas of the world, with very low levels of production and consumption.' Although 70 per cent of its population is engaged in agriculture its productivity is the lowest of all the continents. The African has very little to show for the labour of his hands except a bare subsistence living scraped out of an often infertile soil.

The mineral riches of Africa are not in his control: he merely contributes the labour power and has the galling experience of seeing the results of his labour exported to supply the needs of richer and more diversified economies. The toll of the riches is impressive—96 per cent of the world's industrial and gem diamonds, 69 per cent of cobalt, 63 of gold, 48 of antimony, 37 of manganese, 66 of cocoa and 65 of palm oil. But with all these riches the annual income per head for Africans is but 48 dollars in Tanganyika, 57 in Uganda, 69 in Nigeria, 70 in Sierra Leone, 78 in Kenya and 132 in the Central African Federation. This average, ranging from about £10 a year to £45, is only a rough one: the income of most Africans is certainly well below these averages.[1] Africa is one of the great 'have-nots' of the human scene.

It is, of course, again easy to speculate on what would

[1] Jack Woddis, *Africa: The Roots of Revolt* (Lawrence and Wishart, 1960), p. 210.

have happened to Africa if the white man had not intervened with his techniques and know-how, and his skill in marketing the produce of Africa. There is no reason to assume that Africa would have successfully exploited her riches in the same way—although the pro-African propaganda along this line in Ghana, for instance, would suggest that Africans could have done it all by themselves. There is also no evidence to suggest that the withdrawal now of the white man from every quarter of Africa would immediately result in an upward leap in African standards of living.

What is certain is that the vast gap between the developed societies of the West and the backward societies of Africa is no credit to the colonial powers now retiring politically from the African scene. They did much to lay the foundations of economic and social advance, but the net result is that Africa, as a whole, is still only at the opening stages of transition into the modern age. Aid to Africa is still needed, from whatever quarter it may be offered.

The number of Africas now emerging for the scientist, the archaeologist, the pre-historian and the historian to study was obvious to anyone attending the third conference on African History and Archaeology held in London in July 1961. It used to be thought that the map of Africa before, say, 1840 was an empty space particularly in the middle of Africa: a rim of life round the coast lines and all else blank. The archaeologists and the pre-historians are neatly and accurately disposing of that theory by filling in the areas of knowledge from their investigations of sites. burial grounds, camel trails, trade routes, crop histories, diet and food arrangements. The linguists, too, are busy on their hundreds of different formations of speech amongst the African peoples who lived in pre-history Africa.

I have in front of me 123 papers presented at that conference, and to mention a few of them will indicate something of the intense work going on in the world of African learning:

Archaeology and History of Africa before the 17th century

Pharaoh's Egypt and Negro Africa
Archaeology on the coast of Kenya
Iron age research in Northern Rhodesia and Nyasaland
Influence of Christian Nubia in the Chad area AD 800-1200

The History of Crops in Africa

Origin and distribution of cultivated crops in Africa
The introduction of food plants into Africa by the Portuguese
The introduction of maize into West Africa
Bananas in Africa

Archaeology and History in 17th and 18th centuries

The constitutional history of Ethiopia
Oral traditions in Ruanda and Burundi
Early smoking pipes in West Africa
Trade and politics on the Gold Coast in the 18th century

Trade Routes in pre-Colonial Africa

The caravan trade in the 19th century
A medieval trade route from the Niger to the Gulf of Guinea
Africa's trade with India in the pre-European period
Trade routes in the Congo

Twentieth-century Africa

Africa and America
Tanganyika under British administration
The modern history of the Sudan
Economic change as a factor in Gold Coast history

Africa is proving to be a rich research ground for many

learned disciplines which are opening up a world previously assumed to be destitute of evidence of a historical past. The white man has frequently preened himself on the false belief that real African history began with his coming into the continent, and that up to then there was little to say about Africa's history. It is true that in recorded documents there is little to go on before the eighteenth century and the white man's advent, but the store of 'pre-white Africa' is surprisingly rich, and the conference I have referred to is a sign of the immense gathering of evidence that is going on.

How much of that evidence is concerned with Christianity? In those 123 papers, only one touched on the Christian faith in Africa and that was away back in the ninth century when Christianity already knew that its first great attempt to plant the faith had failed.

It is significant that so many modern books and writers on Africa fail to say anything about the place of Christianity in the continent. The Colonial Correspondent of the London *Times* spent some months touring in Africa during 1960 and wrote six excellent articles of sharp and shrewd insight into African affairs without a breath of mention of the influence (or otherwise) of the Christian faith. I have before me a volume of 250 pages entitled *The United States and Africa,* the report of an Assembly on Africa held at Columbia University, New York, in 1958, which is full of first-rate material and judgment on the African scene from an American point of view. But it contains not one mention of the Christian Church and its place in Africa.

This observers' boycott of the Church is either deliberate or is just an oversight of an institution so taken for granted in African life that to mention it would be superfluous. No one would claim for the Christian Church in Africa that its place is so securely set in African society that the revolution through which Africa is passing will leave its foundations unshaken. No one would claim either that you can write about the history of West, East and Southern Africa without mentioning the Christian Church and the work that it has done in education, medicine, social welfare and its battle for the rights of the African peoples.

Christianity for the last century in Africa has been part of the history of the continent, and more than that. It has made African history. It has shaped African character and life, given new standards of living, offered education and touched the continent's life at every point of its existence. These are bold claims and most of them will be dealt with later in this book. But the question now is whether all this is of the past, something that the archaeologist will one day dig up, and the research historian pore over in the archives?

In the Christian West we have perhaps too lightly assumed that the immense investment of Christian missions in Africa during the last century would automatically reap a harvest that one day would produce a Christian Africa. We have had every right to assume this. The successful propaganda of missionary societies has conditioned our thinking towards Africa and we have had much living evidence of the truth of Christian victory in Africa. Only time, we have been told, was required before the continent would be added to the historic lands of the Christian faith.

We must still believe that, because we believe in the ultimate triumph of the Gospel. But every man's Africa does not mean a Christian Africa in the manner of the West, nor does it mean a continent won for Christ after a pattern conceived by the mission boards of Europe and America. What is in revolution in Africa today is a revolution which cannot leave the Church untouched: if it does, then the Church is failing to be the living instrument of the faith in Africa. The Church must be conditioned by the fierce politics of the time, and be moulded by the effervescent enthusiasms of an awakening continent.

The danger of the Christian community in Africa today

is quiescent aloofness, a withdrawal from the scenes of political life because they appear to be 'dirty' or 'full of graft' or 'un-Christian'. That is the way of death for the Christian Church in Africa or anywhere else.

It may be because the Church in Africa is no longer a formative and influential factor in African life that the historians and journalists either don't see it or, if they do, ignore it. It may be that the Church has ceased to be the directive organization which once supplied the good things of the white man's life to Africa including education, social welfare and a respectable place in society.

Answers to these conundrums are not easy to formulate, but in trying to discover them we shall go very near to finding out how Christianity is faring in a continent where it still has a chance of being a redemptive and reconciling community. I repeat 'still has a chance', for the tides of change are flowing swiftly in Africa and there are many observers who do not think that the Church is moving with them.

2

MAKING UP FOR LOST TIME

AFRICA IS a continent in a hurry. She is making up for time lost in the centuries of unrecorded isolation when her peoples were out of the stream of the world's life.

Divided into hundreds of separate units, or tribes, the continent lacks a cohesive single heritage in history, art, literature or religion to provide a sense of belonging together. Unlike the Asian countries Africa has no cultural or linguistic unity binding large sections of its peoples together. She is now jumping from tribe to nation, and from foreign rule to independence in a few short years, and doing it in a succession of violent leaps with all the world looking on.

What makes a nation? And what is the impetus which gives African nationalism its drive and directive?

There can be no final definition of what goes to make a nation, but chief amongst them must be a common history, customs, language, religion and a way of life that helps to develop a national character and personality. It is true, of course, that nation-making can be accomplished by the arbitrary drawing of a few lines on the map as in the case of Pakistan, and even Nigeria, declaring that to be the birth of a new nation. But the slower processes of common growth in environment, opinion, and a way of life that is recognizable and creative are the ones through which the older nations of Europe, Asia and North America have developed. The negro nations of Africa, now sparking off their revolutions and leaping into independence, have never had these formative experiences except in a common devotion to land, and in the possession of tribal legends which can hardly rank as common history of a nation.

While the great central areas of Africa were not, as was mentioned in the previous chapter, entirely without form and void before the advent of the white man, yet from them did not emerge pride in history, literature, art and religion which have made nations in other countries. What archaeologists and pre-historians are now discovering in those areas are the scattered evidences of a past in certain art forms in painting, sculpture and pottery, but hardly the continuous evidence of independent peoples. In spite of Ghana's propaganda to the contrary, it has to be admitted that the African nations now coming into being are practically brand-new creations which owe the nourishment of their nationalism to other sources, and perhaps one source only.

And that source is a sense of humiliation. This may seem a curiously unpowerful source in which to see the origin of nations, but in Africa's case it arises from the sense of humiliation, 'upon realizing their own retarded position among the peoples of the world'. I owe this clue to African nationalism to Miss Margery Perham's penetrating analysis of it published in *Optima* (November 1960). She says:

> African nationalism—we must use the word for convenience if not with exactitude—should be seen in its earlier stages as the sum of the sense of indignity felt by individuals. The humiliation has not been felt, with one or two possible small exceptions, in the context of anything that could be called a nation. It has been experienced by negro Africans not only separately but also as members of a race, a situation underlined because that race, in colour and form, had such very distinctive features.

Mr Nehru once added a fifth freedom, 'freedom from contempt', to the world's aspirations, a freedom that most aptly fits Africa as well as Asia. Mr Nehru's continent, however, has its own source of pride and culture, and is able to stand on its own ground in unity and independence. But in Africa's case it has been otherwise. Her humiliation and subjection have been profound.

The bitterest humiliation of all was the slave trade and slavery. Britain, quite rightly, takes a pride in its leading part in ridding Africa of the scourge of slave trading which at the depth of its misery, between 1770 and 1807, was pouring 100,000 Negroes a year from the West African coast across the Atlantic to America. But no alibi in the abolition of this traffic in human beings can alter the fact that it dealt a mortal blow to Africa, and helped to depopulate and disintegrate the peoples of central Africa. Slave trading was made easy because of the weakness of the tribal positions, and the occupation of Africa by European powers was made easier still by its effect on the tribes. Here and there a strong tribal-nation like the Ashanti, the Zulu and the Matabele, or the Basuto, put up a resistance to European rule, but by and large Africa submissively accepted European annexation.

But the seeds of humiliation had been sown, particularly in individuals. While the vast mass of the population accepted what the white man brought in roads, railways, lamps, bicycles, new foods, new ideas, schools and religion, those who began to travel outside Africa saw the continent in a new light. They got Western education and at the same time an experience of colour prejudice in the cities of the West; they looked at their Africa, and believed that only independence could give them a position amongst the nations of the world.

Humiliation led to indignation, protest and organization. But this was confined to the educated few who, between the two world wars, met in Europe's student circles and saw their Africa subject to the all-powerful white man. After 1945 with the swift rise in educated groups in West and East Africa the pace of nationalism quickened. 'Colonialism' became a dirty word. The sense of inferiority in being an African brought violent reactions against the white man, and growing demands for a share in the government of their countries. Leaders such as Nkrumah in the Gold Coast set out to educate the masses of the people in ideas of freedom or independence and of throwing off the colonial yoke, and won, hands down, in popular elections.

This is now a familiar and a very recent tale. In a sense the ideas of freedom and independence had to be imported into Africa and one of the most powerful of the importers was the Christian Church with its teaching of the worth of the individual, his place in society, his direct relationship with God, and the infinite value of the human soul. Nearly all the present generation of African leaders had their education in Christian schools and colleges—Nkrumah, Nyerere of Tanganyika, Kenyatta of Kenya, Kaunda of Northern Rhodesia and Banda of Nyasaland to mention only those in the former British areas.

Another of the African leaders, Ndabaningi Sithole of Rhodesia, has told how two South African Bantu were arguing one day about the value of the missionary enterprise to the cause of African nationalism. One was highly critical. 'You see', he said, 'the missionary came here and said, "Let us pray", and we closed our eyes. But when we responded "Amen" at the end of his prayer, we found the Bible in our hands but our land had slipped out of our hands.'

His friend replied in a different vein. 'When Europeans took our country we fought them with our spears, but they defeated us because they had better weapons. And so colonial power was set up. But lo! the missionary came in time and laid explosives under colonialism. The Bible is now doing what we could not do with our spears.'

African nationalism may take surprising turns in its political expressions, but its origins lie in the universal elements of the Christian faith which proclaim the dignity of man, and the quality of men before God.

These beliefs have created some determined political practitioners one of whom, Nkrumah of Ghana, has carved round the plinth of his statue in Accra an adjusted phrase from the New Testament, 'Seek ye first the political kingdom and all other things shall be added unto you'. Politics is all, and in Nkrumah's case, he thinks of the whole of Africa. Politics for him means control and authoritarian ruling. Politics means that the black man has an instrument to establish his right to rule which lifts him out of the slough of subservience to the white man. An earlier, but gentler, propounder of this same political-religious realism was J. K. Aggrey with his famous simile of the black and white notes of the piano making harmony when played together.

On the eve of Ghana's independence I stood looking at the shield of the 'black and white' notes over the doorway of the Achimota School, with which both Aggrey and Nkrumah were associated. 'Will black and white notes go on playing together?' I asked a group of Africans. Two were schoolmasters, three parsons, one a domestic science teacher, and all worked closely with Europeans.

'Well, it's like this,' said one of the schoolmasters. 'We want harmony between black and white. But who is going to play the piano in future? For a long time the white man has been on the piano stool. It's time he got off and let the black man play the tune.' It also occurred to me that it is not impossible to get a tune of sorts out of the black notes by themselves. It may be crude and a bit crazy but it is a tune whose weird assortment of sharps and flats is not un-African to listen to.

But this recognition of the influence of Christianity on African nationalism is also accompanied by a strong revolt against the white man, and this could mean, in extreme instances, the rejection of Christianity itself as was seen in the Mau Mau outbreak in Kenya. Linked traditionally with the white man Christianity must, if it is to grow in Africa, be seen to be truly African and not just an off-shoot of colonial custom. In many of the older Christian areas of Africa, on the west and east coasts, the Christian churches do bear many of the marks of truly indigenous churches. But it is the uncommitted Africa which is rising to power under the sway of nationalism, and Christianity must win this Africa if it is to be the religion of the continent.

The Christian Church itself has to make up for lost time in Africa, and move out of the cocoon of colonialism and be established with a style and image which are recognizably African.

One of the ways of doing this is to let it be seen that the administration of the Church is in African hands: a policy that the Anglican Church in particular has followed most admirably in the last ten years. When Lord Fisher of Lambeth became Archbishop of Canterbury in 1945 there was only one independent Anglican Province in Africa—South Africa, which acquired that status in 1853. It needed a century of tuition and guidance for indigenous Christianity north of the Limpopo River to move into independence—West Africa 1951; Central Africa 1955; East Africa 1960 and Uganda and Ruanda-Urundi 1961. In each case, however, ecclesiastical autonomy preceded the political, and the Church may claim that it helped to prepare men and women for political leadership and self-government.

The Church in general has also proved its ability to live under the various types of political government that are now emerging in Africa including the *apartheid* republic of South Africa, the *centralized* autocracy of Ghana, the *federal* type of government as in Nigeria and *parliamentary* type as in Tanganyika. It is also the Church of territories such as the Bechuanaland Protectorate and Barotseland where *chieftainship* government is still a living factor in political and social life and where the Church, as linked with the chiefs, carries the air of an *established* Church.

In fact the Christian Church must be adaptable to African ways, while preserving the essential doctrines of the Christian faith, and it must speak and worship in a manner that Africa understands. No doubt its failure to do this in the past partially accounts for the hundreds of 'separatist churches' which are strewn across the continent, and will be commented on in a later chapter. They, too, are essentially part of the process of making up for lost time and of the struggle to create an 'African personality' in religion as the politicians, like Nkrumah, are trying to do in politics.

The sense of humiliation as the pace maker in African nationalism is closely accompanied by the experience of 'discrimination' which has been the lot of the majority of Africans when in contact with the white man.

In those pockets of white settlement in East, Central and South Africa the African has been made to feel his second-class position, or as Miss Perham puts it in the *Optima* article referred to, 'the European appears to Africans to be guilty of turning them out of their lowly hut of contentment, or at least of unconsciousness, erecting at its door the glittering house of his own civilization, and then forbidding him entry except to the kitchen and the workshop'.

Felt most bitterly at first by educated Africans, who had attained standards of intellectual achievement often far beyond the average European settled in Africa, the feeling of discrimination has spread through all classes of Africans during the last ten years with the result that nationalism has acquired its fierce 'anti-white man', 'anti-colonial' accent, and the belief that only complete freedom and independence would suffice. Hence the intense hatred of such words as 'partnership' and 'federation' in Central Africa which are regarded as only another subterfuge by the white man to maintain his supremacy, and as less honest than the degraded *apartheid* of the Republic of South Africa.

There is a rough violence in the speed of all this which has shaken many white well-wishers in Africa, and particularly people within the Church who have wanted change to come more gracefully and understandably. All the arguments about how much the white man has done for Africa in investing his money, his skill, his time and indeed his home and himself have been used to stem the tide of change. The dangers of such eruptions of nationalism as seen in Congo have been held up as examples of the terror to come, but the pace of change has not slackened. Political advancement is the key in the door of Africa and the urge to turn it has not been pacified by promises or even by powerful delaying action. Nkrumah's phrase, 'We prefer self-government with danger to servitude with tranquillity', has rung round the continent, in much the same way (ironically enough) as Campbell-Bannerman's 'Good government is no substitute for self-government' did sixty years ago when the (then) Union of South Africa was granted its freedom.

Mr Macleod, then the British Colonial Secretary, had some wise words about this when in January 1961 he spoke to some two thousand British 'sixth formers' in the Central Hall, Westminster. He gave a warning against 'four illusions which could cloud clear thinking about Africa:

1. That if education, housing and health standards were improved, people would stop asking for political advancement.
2. That economic arguments could be decisive. Economic and political advance should go together.
3. That what was suitable for an old established parliamentary democracy like Britain was necessarily suitable for export.
4. That a tiny minority was capable of governing a country more efficiently than the majority of its inhabitants.'

These warnings are strong ones, both to individuals and to every institution and organization which is concerned with an Africa that is making up for lost time. Speed matters; changes that are seen to be changes are demanded. People not ready to accept them are better out of the way, and any institution that is only looking back on the past is doomed to be destroyed or at the best disregarded.

To be disregarded and ignored is worse than opposition and destruction for the Christian Church.

I cannot forget a Sunday afternoon in the township of Harari in Salisbury, Southern Rhodesia. There the St Michael's Mission have built a magnificent new Anglican church, which in its modern stance and lighting is a symbol of the new Africa. On the way to the church I passed a huge meeting near the massive hostels built for migrant labour. It was about politics, beer, wages, 'passes': it was everything to do with life in Africa. Such a meeting fifty years ago would certainly have had a white man or two addressing it and offering advice, and even a missionary on the platform. But not today. The afternoon service at St Michael's had a big congregation of women and children, with a few elderly and middle-aged men at the back. I wondered about the two assemblies and how the gap between them is to be bridged.

Some courageous Christian witness is being given in Central Africa as the speed of redeeming lost time gathers momentum. In the Copper Belt, for instance, Colin Morris has spoken fearlessly to 'both sides'—European and African—from the pulpit of the Chingola Free Church:

> I hope that you can come to like as well as love your African political opponents. How easy it is to be intimidated by that sinister word 'nationalism'. It conjures up visions of some vast, lowering, impersonal force casting a black shadow across Africa. For this reason we must keep firmly in our minds the truth that nationalism is

> *people.* African nationalism is the African people. Some of them are rogues and scallywags, just as some Europeans are rogues and scallywags. But most of them are honest family men, fearful of tomorrow, concerned for their rights, and determined to fight for a society in which the future of their children is secure. Is there not, then, a great basic bond between us?

And to Africans:

> As a European I ask forgiveness for my race. But I remind you that sin is common to all races: the same sins are in all our hearts. You say: the European discriminates against us because we are black. But do not Africans discriminate against each other? Do not the men of this tribe look down upon the men of that one as weak and stupid and poor? You say: the rich Europeans wants nothing to do with the poor African. But does not this rich African who has much wealth or many cattle want nothing to do with those poor Africans who have none of these things? Do not some educated Africans withdraw in pride from their brothers who have little education? These things are in all our hearts, black and white, because we are sinners. And God will only forgive the sins we commit against our brothers of the same race if we are prepared to forgive those of other races who sin against us.

And to both:

> We know that there is not an African Church, nor a European Church. There is only God's Church. . . . It is God's will we should not bring our racial differences before his altar, but that we should be reconciled as one people. A church from which European Christians, whether missionaries or laymen, were shut out would not be a church which worshipped God, but one which worshipped the African. And does not God warn us in the first of His Commandments that He will not tolerate any false Gods? So also a church from which African Christians were shut out would be making a God of the European race. If we

allow this to happen, the judgment upon us will be terrible.[1]

In Kenya a group of Quakers went to see Jomo Kenyatta in June 1961, while he was still in restricted residence at Maralal, and asked him about the future of immigrant races —European and Asian—in a Kenya ruled mainly by Africans.

According to the report published in *The Friend*, London (14 July 1961), he said, 'those who accepted Africans as equal human beings would stay; the others would leave. The master-servant relationship was a bad thing and must disappear entirely. Surely the fears of the immigrant races were based on the assumption that the master-servant relationship would be reversed, that Europeans would be made to serve Africans'. Kenyatta stressed that all that Africans wanted was equality. He thought that there were still Europeans who imagined that the Ham and Shem story was applicable to Kenya in that Africans (the children of Ham) were for ever condemned to be servants of Europeans (the children of Shem). He deplored the use of Bible pictures in which the angels were always white and the devil always black.

In Kenyatta's opinion 'the African Government of the future would have one central aim: to make all citizens equal in the eyes of the law. Was not this is in conformity with the Christian ideal? Were we not all children of one God, who commanded us to love one another? There would be no colour bar, no discrimination in the Kenya of the future. He had been fighting against injustice for over forty years, and it would be painful for him to practise injustice on anyone'.

Time and change are the rhythm in the speeches of all African leaders. They speak from the inside of the revolu-

[1] Colin Morris, *Out of Africa's Crucible* (Lutterworth, 1961), pp. 19, 58, 61.

tion, a well-nigh impossible position for any non-African to assume however favourable he may be to African aspirations. The centuries of humiliation, and the contemporary discriminations, are powerful in the memory and even more so in every-day contacts. Looking at the situation from the calm of his position in the United Nations Economic Commission for Africa, Mr Frederick S. Arkhurst of Ghana says:

> The dynamism of change in Africa and the direction of such change is of great importance not only to Africans but also to all men of goodwill. Africans have the obligation to develop those policies which will command the respect of the world. Our friends in other parts of the world will also have to understand the real and staggering problems which face the peoples of Africa. The time at the disposal of Africans to develop their institutions is very limited, and for decades Africans will need the moral and material assistance of the advanced countries. More important still, the great powers must appreciate that the old order in Africa is dead. Any attempt to delay the process of change or to preserve the *status quo* in Africa cannot but lead to very strained relations between themselves and all Africans.[1]

'The old order in Africa is dead.' Does that include the Christian Church? Every institution in Africa is being looked at with critical eyes: there are no sacred cows sure of protection from the fire and force of a whole continent making up for lost time, and the Christian Church ought not to expect to be free from criticism. There are four chief accusations thrown at the Church as a whole in Africa.

The first of them is the seeming indifference of the Church, as seen in its missions, to have a policy towards the cultural changes in African life. This is often a vague accusation but it can be summed up in this way. Christianity has known what to do about schools, colleges, hos-

[1] *An African Treasury*, p. 63.

pitals, dispensaries and formal preaching in the local congregation. Something of a going concern is seen in action in all those fields, and Africa owes a great debt to Christianity for its gifts to Africa. But in the wider aspects of citizenship, in the sociological issues raised by urban life, rural life, race relationships, and the like, the Church has often appeared to be both powerless and speechless. It has been left to a noble company of individuals to speak for the Christian faith. Looking at the South African race situation Mr Alan Paton told the All-Africa Church Conference at Ibadan, Nigeria (1958):

> Our churches are to a dangerous degree conforming churches, and instead of transforming society, have become conformed to it. There are Christians and churchmen, both lay and clerical, who have refused to conform and who have spoken out against conforming. But, on the whole, in racial matters the South African churches obey the customs of the country rather than the great commandments . . . the Church's duty is not to preserve the *status quo*; its duty is to conserve those supra-temporal foundations on which the *status quo* was based. The people of Africa are on the march into the modern age; and the Church must march with them, the guardian not of what is old but of what is ageless.[1]

The pietistic, keep-free-from-politics, strain in African Christianity is a strong one, and rarely produces Christian leaders who see the relevance of Christianity to the common life. It is perhaps expecting too much of African Christianity itself to produce leadership in a field of Christian enterprise that is still largely untilled even in the West. But the call of the new Africa is for some pioneer Christian sociologists who will help the Church to be livingly identified with the developing culture and customs of the new Africa and, to adapt Alan Paton's words, to be *transformers* of society rather than *conformers* to it.

[1] *The Church in Changing Africa*, p. 54.

This leads to the second criticism which thoughtful Africans levy at the Church and its missionaries—their identity with the West and its civilization, and the tacit assumption that naturally Africa will do best by adopting the West as its pattern. The shadow of Livingstone lies heavily across the continent. His belief that commerce, civilization and Christianity go naturally together has not waned for the European with the passing of the years. But the new African, with his sense of mission to all Africa and his eagerness to create an 'African personality', is not so convinced. Commerce he wants, and civilization too, and he is prepared to do a lot of 'copy book' work in imitating the white man in trade and ways of life.

But religion strikes deeper than all this: it must speak to the soul of Africa and must genuinely 'belong' and not be an 'importation'. The Westernization of Africa is not the goal of most of Africa's political leaders although they will take all the West has to offer in material aid and technical direction and it could appear to them that the Christian Church is the last bulwark of Western domination, a hang-over of the hated colonialism of the old Africa. The Christian Church must become part of the 'image' of Africa contributing its own life and vitality to the 'African personality'. Only time will show whether it has this capacity.

Alongside this view one must recognize some of the inherited handicaps of Christianity in a continent that is rushing so vehemently to make up for lost time.

The association of the Church with 'colonialism' will take long generations to eradicate, all the more so because that association in education and social welfare was in the finest traditions of service to Africa. The Church was the willing agent of state policy, and the handler of state resources to such an extent that few Africans could see where State ended and Church began. In his study of this relationship in East Africa, Dr Roland Oliver concludes that 'however far the doctrines of Christianity and the interests of the Churches might tend towards an upholding of the right and just action of the State, towards the moderation of racial antipathies and towards the avoidance of violence, that influence could only be weakened by the official association of the missions with the State.'[1]

It is, of course, too early yet to make final judgments about this relationship which during the last fifty years has been of inestimable benefit to 'colonial' Africa. The Church believed, in the 1920s, that it was being offered an immense range of opportunity to assist Africa which, with its own resources, it was not capable of meeting. With generous government aid the Church moved especially into the field of education with remarkable success, and established that powerful combination of 'church and school' over large areas of east, west and southern Africa where the British writ ran.

Has the Church paid too heavy a price for that eagerness to co-operate with colonial governments? Has she put far too much emphasis on formal education as governments conceive it, and not enough on her own conception of Christian education in the life of the Church? Would she do it all over again?

These questions are probably unanswerable at the present time for they are the rough, thrusting questions which come from within a revolutionary situation. But they are the ones that Africa is asking of the Church.

A final question, and one which runs all through this kind of argument in Africa, is the one often poised by Africans that they have rarely been given their rightful chance in the direction of missions and church. Sir Francis Ibiam, one time Principal of the Hope Waddell Institution at Calabar, and now Governor of Eastern Nigeria, put this

[1] Roland Oliver, *The Missionary Factor in East Africa* (Longmans, 1952), p. 285.

point in speaking at the East Asia Christian Conference in 1959:

> Some missionaries do not want to build up indigenous churches at all. Some do not believe in what they call 'new-fangled ideas and methods'. And others cannot bear to see power—administrative or monetary power—pass out of their hands and reach. To us who are African born and very happy to belong to Africa, we cannot understand such a philosophy. One can readily understand this philosophy coming from an incorrigible and diehard imperialist or an insatiable and greedy capitalist with monopoly rights and business tentacles everywhere and all over the place doing everything in his power, wise or foolish, to make Africa stay put. But not an avowed Christian—one who has dedicated himself before God to a life of missionary service.

The missionary as *bwana,* as master, has been part of the African scene for a hundred years and more, but like all other African personalities and institutions he is being closely scrutinized and criticized. Most missions and missionaries have talked loudly and sincerely about 'devolution' and 'handing over' responsibility to Africans, but many of them have also deeply doubted the wisdom of it, and have managed in so many places to remain in the saddle of control. It would be a genuine tragedy for Christianity in Africa if 'the missionary' were to be the last white man in authority, the last relic of the old order in Africa, the one who had to be thrust out by political events rather than the one who anticipated events and showed his greatness by being follower instead of leader.

Fortunately there are many examples all over Africa where 'the missionary' has in the New Testament sense become 'the servant' and has been the active promoter of the devolution process. In a large number of instances he has been ahead of his Africa, egging on a reluctant Church to the stage of independence, reminding it to make up for lost time, and often disappointed at the response. Like 'colonialism', 'mission' and 'missionary' are now targets for all in Africa and deserve some of the shooting. A fair judgment on them has yet to come.

3

TRAMP OF A CONTINENT

AFRICA IS a restless place: it is always on the move. The myriad little trackways which cover the land surface are padded out by the steady barefooted tramp of the women carrying water, the men going to palavers, the herd-boys out to the cattle. What seems to be an everlasting calm under the heavy heat is a deceptive peace. The forest stirs to the lumber men, the cocoa farmers, the palm oil men; the bush suddenly gives way to mine compounds and the air is loaded with the deep thud of machinery. Even when you stand still on a deep jungle trackway to sample its primeval peace there will be a crackle of snapping twigs, and down the pathway will come a traveller with his blanket rolled on his shoulder, as he passes on with a smile of greeting, steadily tramping out the miles in his bare feet.

It has been like that in Africa for thousands of years, and the pattern in some parts is little changed. But in the last twenty years Africa has shown a new restlessness, and has given itself some mighty heaves.

I remember being taken on a visit to his native village by a distinguished Nigerian lawyer, an Ibo man of Onitsha, and a member of the English Bar at Gray's Inn. We left his car on the main road and began to walk along the intricate trackways, he in his black coat and waistcoat, striped trousers and stiff collar, and I in a pair of shorts and an open-necked shirt. Deeper and deeper into the forest went the track, one of those endless mazes of almost invisible communication that only a local man could follow.

The village itself was locked in a mass of tall palm trees, each family within its own stockade of thatched huts, all ingeniously camouflaged into a green and brown mosaic. In one courtyard, wizened, naked, but still upright and dignified, was the lawyer's grandmother. The salt of welcome was scattered, the cola beans were handed round and the old lady grinned at her grandson and his companion from a world she had heard about but hardly, perhaps, believed existed. Illiterate, primitive, seven thousand years old in customs, One Africa met the other which went down on its knees (striped trousers and all) to kiss the old lady's hand.

You don't ever need to go to Africa to be aware that it is a continent on the move. If your map of Africa is pre-1960 beware of using it, for in that year black Africa, from the bend of the bulge in the west to the heart of the south-central in Congo, shook itself free from a century of colonialism and put fifteen independent countries on the map.

What used to appear on the maps as the purple of France, the red of Britain and the yellow of Belgium gave way to a myriad variety of coloured flags which waved over lands and territories that had said farewell to the white man's authority and welcomed in the rule of Africans.

The very names of these countries are a reminder of Africa's infinite variety of terrain. There are the sub-Sahara countries of Mauritania, Mali, Niger and Chad; the west coast countries of Nigeria, Senegal, Ivory Coast, Upper Volta, Dahomey, Cameroun, Gabon, Togo and Congo Republic; the central countries of the Republic of Central Africa, and Congo. Add to them two outliers in the east—Somalia and Madagascar, and 1960 takes its place on the roll of the great years of freedom. Previous to 1960, Ghana, Guinea, Morocco, and Tunisia led the way, joining Libya, Egypt, Sudan, Ethiopia and the Republic of South Africa in independence. These new nations were followed in 1961 by Sierra Leone and Tanganyika, with the Cameroons making its plebiscite decision to divide and join Nigeria and Cameroun. They have now been joined by Algeria, Uganda, Rwanda and Burundi.

But considering areas of Africa are still wrestling with the shape of their things to come. The British related territories of the Rhodesias and Nyasaland, Kenya, Gambia and Bechuanaland, Swaziland and Basutoland; the Portuguese colonies of Guinea, Angola and Mozambique; the Spanish Rio Muni and Rio de Oro; and French Somaliland—all are at various stages on the road to independence, with some hardly started.

From a continent of colonies, Africa has become a continent of some fifty countries whose political characters are not always after the manner of their former colonial overlords. One-party government is the rule in most of the newly independent countries and we must be prepared for shocks to our democratic conceptions of government as the African political personality develops. Their leaders have had to force the pace of their country's march to independence with vehemence, and with much propaganda, and the same requirements are needed now to maintain the momentum and to keep them in power. Their leaders speak constantly of the need for 'strong government', which in the eyes of Western democrats looks much like 'fascism' with the leaders using their internal power for external purposes and 'imperial' dreams colouring their speeches. And at the southern tip of Africa a white minority is building up a type of one party government based on a white racist theory which is only strengthening the 'fascist' tendencies in black Africa.

Western democracy, with its finely balanced parties managing a governmental machine by discussion and popular votes, is obviously not for Africa as a whole. The British in particular, in their eagerness to export parliamentarianism with its traditional trappings of parliament house, Speaker, mace, government and opposition benches, have failed to perceive that once the bonds of tutelage were cast off Africa would manage its political affairs differently.

The tramp of the map men and the politicians is part of that deeper movement of the peoples in Africa within their own continent which is characteristic of Africa.

Black men, like white men when seen in the mass, all look much the same at a superficial glance. They are usually called Negroes, easily recognized by their dark brown skin and woolly hair. But the Negro, while the largest, is only one of the racial stocks of Africa. According to C. G. Seligman's *Races of Africa* there is evidence for their existence as far back as 3000 BC and their homeland is an area in the great western bulge of Africa. There they met the powerful invading group of Hamites from the east who came into Africa, perhaps via the Horn, from Asia or Arabia. The intermingling of Hamite blood with the other African races had a profound effect on the population of Africa. It helped to produce the Egyptians, the Abyssinians, the Berbers and Tuareg of North Africa, and mixed with Negro blood, it produced that other great section of Africans, the Bantu who moved out of the west into central and southern Africa. The Hamites also mixed with the Bushmen of southern Africa to produce the Hottentots of South Africa, the first Africans to face the inroads of permanent white settlers.

'The civilizations of Africa,' says Dr Seligman, 'are the civilizations of the Hamites, its history the record of these peoples and their interaction with the two more primitive African stocks, the Negro and the Bushman.' It was from the Great Lakes region of the central-north that the Bushman and then the Bantu (offspring of Negro and Hamite) pushed southwards until they occupied the vast domain from north of the Zambesi to the Cape. There the countless tribal groupings of the Bantu people fanned out across what is now the Rhodesias, the Portuguese territories, Bechuanaland, the Transvaal, Natal, the Orange Free State and parts of Cape Colony. By what date they had accomplished this immense, age-long safari it is impossible to say, but two experts have ventured some generally accepted predictions. Dr Monica Wilson believes that by AD 1300 the southward trek of the Bantu peoples was pretty well accomplished and that they were settling down in their new southern homelands, and Professor Schapera holds that, to take an example from the Bantu-Bechuana, they were fixed in their modern recognizable habitats by AD 1600.

The next great movement of the tribes is much more exactly dated. It was the movement that began in what is now Natal between the Drakensberg and the sea under the impetus of the great Zulu Chief, Chaka, between the years 1816 and 1823. His imperial domination, combined with a greed for land and cattle, propelled thousands of Zulu peoples as refugees across the high mountains into the fertile open lands of the Orange Free State and Transvaal to begin those amazing treks which finally in 1838 brought the all-conquering Matabele into Southern Rhodesia, the Makololo into the Zambesi-Chobe basin, and the Angoni into the region of Lake Nyasa. Accompanied by hordes of cattle, and their women and children, the tribes fought and raided their way to the north leaving behind a trail of misery amongst the Bantu which is still not forgotten in tribal memory in southern Africa.

We know a good deal of this movement of the African peoples because it flooded up to the front doors of the pioneer mission station on the frontier of Cape Colony at Kuruman where Robert Moffat had established himself and the Gospel at their 'farthest north' point. There in 1823 he helped to fight off the marauders and save his pastoral Bechuana from the worst of their devastations. This was the last of the major movements of the African tribes and was completed in 1837 when the Boer farmers from Cape

Colony clashed with the Matabele in the Transvaal, and with their guns dispatched them on the last trek across the Limpopo into Southern Rhodesia. The white man was now thoroughly joining in the life of the restless continent.

When did the white man *begin* to join in? For centuries, until practically our own time, Africa was for the white man a coast-line rather than a continent. Before the death of Prince Henry the Navigator (AD 1460), the Portuguese had reached the Rio Grande south of Gambia on the west coast. Twenty-four years later the estuary of the Congo was sighted, and three years afterwards Bartholomew Diaz got to the Cape. In 1498 Vasco de Gama saw Natal. On both coasts, east and west, the Portuguese displayed their skill as navigators and coastal traders and, if they have done little in modern times as colonial administrators, Africa owes a debt to them for their introduction of some of its staple food crops: maize, yams, cassava, sweet potato, sugar-cane, peppers, ginger, citrus—most of which they brought from Brazil not to feed Africans but to feed themselves on the coasts of Africa!

Then came the Dutch, Danish, Spanish, French and British, lured for centuries to the creeks and lagoons of the west coast and the harbours of the east by the lucrative slave trade with little penetration of the interior except for the few Portuguese merchants who traded their beads and cloth for gold and ivory up the Zambesi to the kingdom of Monomotapa, on the borders of modern Southern Rhodesia, in the 1560s. In the south the ultimate boundary of the known African world was, for the Dutch and the British, the Orange River. Not until 1799 did William Anderson, a missionary of the London Missionary Society, cross it for the first time.

One date in the white man's penetration of southern Africa is specially important. In 1652 the Dutch East India Company, under Jan van Riebeck, established a supply depot for their ships at the Cape of Good Hope and thus began the reign of the Dutchman, and eventually the Afrikaner, in southern Africa. Then after the Napoleonic Wars Britain established her sway at the Cape but again valued it chiefly as a port of call for her East Indiamen, and as a military station within the orbit of her far more important Indian Empire. But the white man had come to stay at the salubrious tip of the continent where he found its wheat farms, orchards and vineyards very much to his liking. There was an ample supply of docile labour, some of it slave and some of it Hottentot and Coloured. Away beyond the Colony borders roamed the savage hordes of the Bantu races in an Africa unknown and deeply feared.

Another formative date is 1835-6, when the Great Trek of the Boer farmers gathered its momentum and spilled out of the cosiness of Cape Colony into the domains of Natal, the Orange Free State and the Transvaal. Born out of a mixed parentage—hatred of British rule, dislike of emancipation, hunger for land and space—the Great Trek is one of the major events in Africa's many peregrinations. It brought the white man for the first time in sharp clash with the Bantu peoples, and spread the doctrine of inequality of black and white, in Church or State, across the South African veld.

The trek-farmers carried their *apartheid* beliefs into the making of the new republics of the veld where the native tribes were only tolerated as a plentiful supply of cheap farm labour. To say that these peoples had political rights, as the crass English missionaries did, was bad enough, but to found that belief on the Christian religion was doubly iniquitous in the farmers' eyes. The idea that the Christian religion could change the status of the heathen savage in any way was contrary to the Boer farmer's conception of the faith, and further to preach the strange idea of the equality of all men was misguidedly to mix religion with politics.

From the days of the Great Trek until now, that stern

Boer argument has riddled southern Africa with an interminable debate.

From sailing round the coasts of Africa, as he had done for four hundred years, the white man now had his eyes on the unknown interior, but not until Livingstone prised open the unknown did the march of the white man really move in earnest. His astounding tramp across Africa from Angola to Mozambique, and his last journeys through Tanganyika and Northern Rhodesia to the Great Lakes, filled in the blank spaces on the African map and gave the signal for the white man in his various guises of missionary, traveller, trader, government official, prospector and empire maker to move in. Livingstone's travel years from 1853 to 1873 were the years of the single-hearted missionary-explorer who saw a continent and a people worth saving from internal strife through the advent of the white man and what he might do for Africa. There followed him large numbers of people from the Western world, eager to implement his vision of Africa, who got down to the hard, dogged business of laws, roads, health, food, language, schools, medicine, trade, government: the work on which the independent countries of Africa are now building.

Sir Philip Mitchell, one time governor of Uganda and Kenya, summed up the African situation before the white man in the official report on *Land and Population in East Africa* (C.O. 290, 1952) in this way:

> They (the Africans) had no wheeled transport and . . . no animal transport either; they had no roads nor towns; no tools except small hand hoes, axes, wooden digging sticks, and the like; no manufactures, and no industrial products except the simplest domestic handiwork; no commerce as we understand it and no currency, although in some places barter of produce was facilitated by the use of small shells; they had never heard of working for wages. They went stark naked or clad in the bark of

> trees or the skins of animals; and they had no means of writing even by hieroglyphics, nor of numbering except by their fingers or making notches in a stick or knots in a piece of grass or fibre; they had no weights or measures of general use. Perhaps most astonishing of all to the modern European mind they had no calendar nor notation of time. . . . Before European occupation there was no way of saying '1st January 1890' or '2.30 p.m.', or their equivalents in any language spoken from Abyssinia to the Transvaal, except Swahili along the coast. . . .
>
> They were pagan, spirit or ancestor propitiators in the grip of magic or witchcraft, their minds cribbed and confined by superstition. . . . They are a people who in 1890 were in a more primitive condition than anything of which there is any record in pre-Roman Britain.

In that context the great leap forward of Africa in the last seventy years is all the more remarkable and shows what Africans can do by imitating the ways of other people. How short is the time in Africa, and how restless the people once awakened from the passivity of the centuries, and how much remains to be done!

Reflections such as these afflict everyone who contemplates the continent and its needs today, but in surveying the last fifty years of the white man's association with Africa there are three formative movements which have had and still have their massive effect on the continent.

The first is the tramp to knowledge. Africa's thirst to know and learn has been the outstanding feature of its life during the last fifty years. Linked with the Christian Church, the school has been the shining symbol of progress. I remember the pride with which an old Ghana Methodist pastor took me through his villages with their packed schoolrooms of lively children, and as I afterwards watched the children tramping along the trackways homewards with their exercise books, inkpots and pens admirably balanced on their curly heads I realized that here was the revolution that had more profoundly shaped Africa than any other. Go down any main road in Africa and you will see the pattern of church and school repeated every few miles, the buildings usually the best the village has to show.

It is understandable that the first concerted plan of the African governments of countries like Ghana and Nigeria is to launch an educational drive from primary schools to universities, and to do it with a breathless enthusiasm and with profound belief in the magic word 'education'. When the fine buildings of the University of Ghana were being put up on Legon Hill I stood watching some of the operations and remarked to my companion on the spaciousness and even splendour of it all. 'Yes,' he said, 'this is their temple.'

But what is 'education'? No word has been more mishandled in Africa, or more examined in the heady rush to have it. The fact that the African boy who has got into a secondary school is usually a good examinee, mopping up his certificates with sometimes astonishing ease, has suggested to Africans that this is education. The amassing of enough knowledge through the required text books 'to pass', and the pride in attaining the minimum amount of book-learning have appeared to be 'education'.

In 1951-2 the British Colonial Office carried out what was probably its most exhaustive enquiry into education in the (then) 'British territories in tropical Africa.' It started off with two criticisms in the minds of the enquirers. 'One was that there was too little education: too few children had any chance of any schooling at all, and of those few, too small a proportion carried their schooling to the stage at which it would be really useful to them. The other criticism was that education was effective in breaking up the old African life, but not in adapting its pupils to the conditions of the new. It was bookish, divorced from reality, and gave its pupils a distaste for manual work and rural life.'[1]

Education is at the heart of the restless revolutions in Africa's life, and Africa wants more and more of it. The

[1] *Education in Africa* (HMSO, 1953), p. 5.

tramp to the school is now matched by the tramp to the college. All nine of the university colleges in Africa south of the Sahara have attained their present status since World War II, and five of them are in former British territories. All told, including colleges in Ethiopia, Cairo, Khartoum and the Republic of South Africa, there are twenty institutions of university status open to Africans, with 5,000 students in them. But another 7,000 prefer to go abroad, chiefly to the United Kingdom, for their higher education. Nigeria boasts of 22,000 university graduates; Congo can muster only a dozen, and graduated its first two students only in 1960.

When Billy Graham asked the students of the University of Ibadan in Nigeria how many were products of Christian mission schools every hand was raised. That could happen almost anywhere in Africa, for in the last fifty years the Christian mission for many Africans has meant school and education. Africans acknowledge their indebtedness, but how far that indebtedness will continue into the higher ranges of education in Africa remains to be seen. There are student Christian organizations in most of the colleges, chapels of much dignity (where on any college campus in the world is there a finer chapel than the one at Ibadan?), groups who will meet to discuss in wide generality about religion in Africa, and divinity faculties which are part of the official college organization. But is the Christian religion the driving force of higher education in Africa? Is it the integrating factor which is moulding the character of the graduates who eagerly bend over their books and endure the solid grind of passing examinations in a wide field of knowledge?

Mr Joseph Kiano of Kenya, in his book *Africa is Here,* comes very near to the central issue in African higher education:

> When you say someone is an educated African you mean that he is conscious of his people's problems, that he

knows his culture well enough to be able to discriminate between its drawbacks and its advantages, that he can take the land his people have, the livestock people keep, the wisdom his elders teach, and the customs that his people follow, and, integrating all these with his Western knowledge and techniques, help to construct progressive African communities (p. 30).

It is salutary to recollect that the march of Africans to college is not confined to Africa only, and that the direction of Africa's educated leadership is not settled only on the campuses in Africa but in London, New York and Moscow, where African students are knocking on the doors of knowledge in mounting numbers.

The second formative movement is the tramp to industry. In the short space of fifty years Africa has leaped from a continent of the *machette* and the digging stick to one of mechanical mining and hydroelectric power. These wizardries of the white man set going the steady tramp to industry, to the mines, to the factories, to the power plants and their industrial offsprings in the cities. It is the revolution that touches the life of the ordinary African whether he is bush born, and bush bred, or a gamin of the streets of Lagos or Nairobi.

I remember watching a long line of stately women carrying the red earthen slag on the open-cast tin mines of Nigeria in huge calabashes on their heads, tramping up the slopes of the tips, tipping and running down the other side. They looked like a frieze of Pharaoh's slaves building a temple. A ponderous drag-crane swung a Wellsian steel shovel into mid-air, and thundered it down into the resisting earth with the crunch of a high explosive bomb: clawing, rattling and finally angrily scooping up a mouthful of the tin-loaded earth for the crusher. An invisible European hand high up in the crow's nest cabin of the crane directed the monster. That was ten years ago. Today there is a black hand on the levers of many mining contrivances in Africa both above and below ground, as the mines policy of 'African advancement' gives the African his place amongst the skilled in industry.

The most famous example of industrial impact on African life is the Copper Belt of Northern Rhodesia, which must now be the most investigated and reported on area of the whole of Africa. It is hardly forty years old, and now in its various townships has an African population of over 200,000 with twenty-five per cent of its African workers having done three to six years in the mines, and twelve per cent having served over ten years. There is an air of permanence about its townships with their churches, libraries, schools, beer-halls and a range of houses which however crude they may look in their regimented rows are at least an improvement on the first efforts of the mines to house their workers. Workers are encouraged to bring their families with them, and the single worker saves up to marry a 'home girl' and bring her to the township to live.

The Northern Rhodesian pattern of mining life for the African is strikingly different from the South African traditional methods of recruitment of contract labour. I once spent a day in the African compound of the de Beers diamond mines at Kimberley where in a vast, hygienic and handsomely equipped hostel compound the young Basutos and Bechuana are immured for nine to twelve months of their contract term. The mine management proudly claim that they do not recruit labour because there are always more men seeking work than they can hope to employ, and over seventy per cent of the men return for further periods of contract labour. It is the same at the new gold fields in the Orange Free State where the native hostels provide for all the wants of a mineworker on condition that his work is satisfactory and that he abides by the regulations of the companies.

All this, of course, is within the colonial pattern of

labour. Africans have cracked open the Church and its direction, have moved into the higher realms of education and scholarship, entered the world of medicine and hospitals and government administration. They provide Prime Ministers, and Governor Generals, but big industry in its management and responsibility has yet responsibly to open its doors to Africa. There are all sorts of reasons against this in the white man's mind: 'the African lacks the needed skills'; 'the African is not a good business man'; 'the African lacks responsibility'; 'the African's capital is too small for big business'; 'the white man has every right to hold on to what his brains and skill have developed'.

There is much truth in these statements, and there is much evidence to support them in looking at the *third* of our formative movements, *the tramp to city life*. The African is drawn to the urban areas by money and high wages. We must not exaggerate this drift because it has not yet finally tipped the balance of Africa's life which is still largely rural. But the drift is increasing. Over a five-year period the towns of Southern Rhodesia showed a fifty per cent increase in their African population.

With high wages and money goes a money economy and all the things that money can buy. An African working class has developed which is dependent on the white man's economy and the standards of living which the white man's skill has injected into African life. The cities and towns round which the African townships develop in territories like the Rhodesias, Kenya and South Africa are the white man's towns, and it is for him that the African works on the railways, roads, docks and airfields. He is in transport in order to distribute manufactured goods sent in from the West for sale on African markets. In hotels, clubs and private houses the African is servant, and it is he who often manages the white man's home and sees to his children at all stages of their lives.

The drift to the towns and the gradual urbanization of a lot of African life has in many ways strengthened the colonial dependence of the African. He is no longer the free man of his village community, and often looks back with a certain nostalgia on the old ways of rural life. He is dependent on movements of economy and world trade which he does not understand, and must take on the word of the white man. He is locked into a complex community where he has no roots and where the masters of the scene are mine managers, town managers and the like—men who manipulate life, however efficiently, from offices which do not pretend to have the welfare of African workers as their first concern.

But when all this is recognized, and the move towards the city lights of Africa is examined dispassionately, it must be admitted that this is the Africa of the future. A working class African will move (and is moving) into becoming the middle-class African owning his own house and bringing up his family entirely in an urban area with no roots back home in the bush. Here live the politicians, the pace-makers of African life and the managers of Africa's future economy. This is the world of challenge to the Christian Church which has learned some of the 'know-how' of rural Africa and must now learn how to live and develop in urban Africa.

The cry of an educated, urban African, 'In the village I was a better man', is more than a nostalgic hang-over. It is the cry of a new world in Africa to come over and help.

4

CHRISTIANITY ON ITS METTLE

CHRISTIANITY IS on its mettle in Africa today if only for the historical reason that it is now making its third bid to root itself into African soil.

The first attempts made in the Apostolic Age in Egypt resulted in expansion down the Nile valley into Abyssinia, and what remains of that expansion is seen in the Coptic churches in Egypt and Abyssinia.

But it was in the Roman colonies of North Africa, where today the nations of Morocco, Algeria, Tunisia and Libya are rising, that between AD 180 and AD 430 the Christian Church flourished in some splendour with hundreds of bishops at the height of its greatness and with men such as Tertullian, Cyprian and Augustine to add lustre to its name.

Why did this African Church fail? A great deal of historical research has gone into this problem. This strip of the North African coast was the favoured granary of the Roman Empire with ease of communications to and from Rome, and no doubt the Church had the marks of a colonial Church, but the chief charge against it is that it failed to be a missionary Church, and spent its life-blood on internal controversies.

In its early years, in the second century AD, this African Church won fame for its steadfastness under persecution and the number of its martyrs but it failed to penetrate into the life of the indigenous peoples and won its largest successes with the Romanized top layer. Latin was the dominant tongue and no attempt was made to translate the scriptures into the Berber language. It seems that there was no preaching in it.

When Rome fell in AD 410 the Vandals (*Arian* Christians) moved into power in North Africa with their hatred of both Rome and Catholic Christianity, and not until the sixth century, under the Emperor Justinian, did the Church in North Africa recover some of its ancient splendour. By then it was thoroughly Roman and imperial, with few genuine roots amongst the Berber people to weather the coming Islamic storm.

As the fire of the new power of Islam rose in Arabia and spread through Egypt and North Africa, so the Christian churches gradually succumbed not so much to continuous persecution but to assimilation, apostasy, taxation pressure and Islamic infiltration of their life. In Egypt a remnant proved faithful and are seen in the Coptic churches of today, but in North Africa the Church vanished.

Islam was triumphant because it besieged a community of Christians that had not been sure enough of its Gospel to carry it with confidence and success amongst the indigenous peoples of North Africa. Islam had this confidence and moved powerfully amongst the Berber people thus cutting through any roots that Christianity had in those pagan areas. The Christian Church had become an in-grown urban community without the vision of a Christian Africa beyond the bounds of the old Roman colonial area. In the centuries from AD 200 to AD 700 Christianity missed its supreme chance of expansion in the immense land empire, from the North African coast to the tenth parallel of Latitude North, where today Islam is dominant through its own missionary zeal.

Defeated by itself and by Islam in its first African venture, Christianity had to wait until the fifteenth century for the second attempt. This was made by the Portuguese—down the Guinea Coast mainly in what is now Ghana and

Congo, and in the next century along the eastern coast in Mozambique and as far inland as the borders of modern Southern Rhodesia. But again this venture was mainly a colonial one in which the African coastal chiefs embraced Christianity, and consented to mass baptisms of their people because it was politically expedient. The Jesuits were active in Angola and the Dominicans in Mozambique, where they established Christian villages and schools and sent some of their promising young men to Portugal for further education. Much of this was a cloak for the Portuguese participation in the slave trade, and because of this deserved to fail. In any case there was no depth in the Christian soil.

As the Portuguese moved their interests to the Far East, so this Christian bid for Africa withered along the west and east coasts, leaving inadequate and ill-equipped Christian groups in cities such as Loanda and Mozambique. As on the north, so on the east and west coasts, Christianity failed because it appeared incapable of making itself a religion of the indigenous peoples, and lacked the leadership which might have achieved this.

This brings us to the modern period, and the third attempt of the Christian Church to plant itself on the African continent which had to wait until the missionary awakening in the West of the early nineteenth century, and the urge to do something for Africa which accompanied the abolition of slave trading and the later emancipation movement. It is not possible here to enter into a detailed account of the various mission enterprises which have now given Christianity a firm root in the soil of Africa in large areas south of the Sahara, and which, unlike the previous efforts, are not dependent on colonial overlordship for their sustenance. Historically the divide is roughly pre-Livingstone and post-Livingstone. Up to his arrival in Southern Africa in 1841, Christianity had moved only a short distance north of the Orange River. On the west coast there were only the faint beginnings of the Christian Church, and the east had to wait until 1846 for the pioneer journeys of the German missionaries sponsored by the Church Missionary Society in London.

It was Livingstone's impact which opened the heart of the continent, and after his death in 1873 the missionary enterprise in central Africa leaped ahead. We are living at the end of that period, and therefore are in a position to look critically at the Christian achievement, and see why it is that Christianity after a hundred years of life in Africa is now on its mettle.

In the next chapter I try to answer the question, 'How Christian is Africa?'. Here I want to look at some of those forces with which Christianity now has to do battle. They are are not unlike the ones which it had to face in previous attempts in Africa, and before which it gradually withered away.

First, *Islam*. Christianity's old opponent in the north is now Christianity's contemporary antagonist in many other parts of Africa far to the south of the Sahara-Sudan belt where its power lies. In almost every urban area of southern Africa there are groups of Muslims with their mosques, their marketing, their trading. In Capetown there are said to be 65,000 Muslims, and in the English-tradition city of Durban a splendid blue stucco mosque overshadows the main street of the downtown area. On the birthday of Mohammed the faithful pack the town hall for their celebrations and expect the city's mayor to grace the occasion.

Islam is up and coming all over Africa. The mosque, the fez, the Koranic school, the Muslim trader are ubiquitous symbols of the flowing tide which in some parts of West Africa is said to be bringing converts to Islam in ten times the volume of converts to Christianity.

Statistics are misleading in connection with Islam because nobody really knows its strength, but no one can deny that

Islam is on the offensive in Africa especially in those lands beyond its traditional frontiers and at a time when it appears to fit the political pattern.

Oddly enough the so-called Christian colonial powers, such as Britain and France, protected Islam, in the days of their overlordship, from any thorough approach by Christian missions. The customary machinery of Christian missions was forbidden to operate in Muslim territory—with some rare and special exceptions in Northern Nigeria—with the result that the Islamic strongholds are still intact and well equipped to be the base of Islamic penetration into those areas where Christianity is now losing its prestige value as the white man departs. Islam is there, African to its tips, ready to fill in the vacuum.

It is this 'Africanism' of Islam which is so attractive. In whatever part of the continent it may be, Islam acts as a bond between separated peoples, providing an African culture that is not borrowed from the West. The powerful propagandist of the United Arab Republic is continually playing the catching tune—'Africa is Black, Islam is Black'.

Much of this 'Pan-Africanism', and cultural Muslimism, is not directed against Christianity as a religion although the prophets who move southwards from Cairo are not slow to point out to Africans the weakness of Christianity as a religion for Africa. What is being built up is a kind of 'cultural pluralism' with toleration for various religions. This might provide a more favourable climate for Christian witness, but again it might not. I get the impression that this is the situation in Western Nigeria, where in the Yoruba country Christianity is certainly on its mettle as it faces the silent, almost unobtrusive, penetration of Islam.

The religious attractions of Islam are many to the uncommitted pagan African. He does not, perhaps, sit down formally and examine the differences between Islam and Christianity, but he is 'aware' of the former being *first* thoroughly African in its ways. If a trader-proselytizer comes into his village one African speaks to another in a way that certainly no white man, and not many Westernized Christian Africans, can ever do. Social life, trade, worship and religious customs are all of one piece for the Muslim and he shows it in his conduct.

This sense of social unity is the *second* factor in Islam's advance. There is no break for the convert. If he should be a polygamist he does not have to make critical decisions about his way of life which affect not only him but other people dependent on him. He does not flounder in the customs of an alien religion, his children go to a Koranic school and there talk an African language, Arabic, instead of the white man's English.

Thirdly, the agents of Islam move within the trading and social context of African life and meet the people where they live in their homes and especially in the markets. The Arabic trader, lively, talkative and ubiquitous, is a figure of African life in a manner that the African Christian pastor has never achieved: when a series of paintings were issued for Nigerian independence the Muslim trader appeared in nearly all of them. Islam's pervasive infiltration has been accomplished without that professional clericalism which, to many people, is one of the worst impositions of the Christian West on Africa.

One active section of Islam, the Ahmadiyya Muslim Movement directed from Pakistan, has, however, paid Christianity the compliment of borrowing some of its methods. This sect of Islam, which is increasingly active in Sierra Leone and along the west coast, has three purposes, to reform and purge Islam, to express Islam in a way understood in the modern world, and to 'answer the challenge of Christianity both by copying and borrowing from Christian faith and practice and by seeking their overthrow.' It goes in for schools of the modern kind, imports missionaries for evangelistic work and is now starting medical missions.

Is Africa South to be the scene of a struggle between Cross and Crescent for the allegiance of uncommitted pagan Africa? The question provides the key to the continent. There are those who argue that the transition from pagan tribalism to the austerities and disciplines of Christianity is too drastic for large numbers of Africans, and that Islam could provide a half-way house, a kind of preparation for Christianity. They say that the Islam of Africa South is not the Islam of Africa North, and that the two religions can live side by side, even ministering to one another through the dialogue of discussion and mutual understanding.

All this sounds comforting and attractive for the Christian Church in Africa South, but the writing on the wall of African Christian history provides a grim warning. There is no alibi for the missionary purpose of the Church, and no substitute for making the Gospel and the Church indigenous to the life of a people.

I cannot forget once attending a meeting of the Ghana Christian Council in the handsome Community Centre in Accra which has glass walls. It was a Friday. As the morning wore on to noon I could see the Muslim workers of the city assembling on the pavements which surrounded the hall until eventually the Christian meeting appeared to be besieged by solid groups of Muslims with their heads bowed towards Mecca. The penetrating, enveloping power of Islam has already shown what it can do in Africa both with Christian and Pagan communities. History never repeats itself exactly, but with Islam in Africa South it could come ominously near it.

Secondly, Christianity is on its mettle in Africa because it has to face the obloquy of *racism*. I know of no other word which really fits the peculiar dilemma that Christianity is in. On the one hand it is the religion with the clearest assertion of the brotherhood of men as set out in the Epistle to the Galatians with its oft trumpeted, 'There is neither Jew nor Greek, there is neither slave nor free, there is neither male nor female; for you are all one in Christ Jesus' (Gal. 3.28). On the other it is the religion which so often, and seemingly permanently, denies this claim in practice.

The taunt of being a racist religion is a hard one for Christianity to bear but we have to admit the truth of it in most areas of Africa where the white man, especially of Anglo-Saxon stock, lives in close proximity to the Bantu. The white man goes on his way to *his* Christianity, and the black man goes a separate way to *his* Christianity. Racism has entered into the blood stream of Christianity in Africa dividing a common religion into two compartments of people who use the same formula of faith and practise the same worship but do it separately.

This is seen in all its depressing rigidity in the Republic of South Africa where the dominant Dutch Reformed Churches are deeply involved in the Afrikaner ideology of race which asserts the supremacy of the white race, and the ordained necessity of maintaining it in Church and State. Who or what ordains has never been made clear by the Dutch Reformed Churches since an attempted justification for *apartheid* in Christianity by fiddling with certain Biblical texts and contexts has now largely been abandoned.

In his remarkable analysis of the South African situation *No Further Trek,* Dr P. V. Pistorius of Pretoria University says:

> While the Church stood on the fact of the diversity of peoples and nations, they could cover their point by saying that God willed separate nations and peoples and that the principle would have to be applied at all costs in the Church also. *But once the starting-point became the Church, there was the unescapable fact that the unity of the Church would have to be demonstrated in some way* (p. 63).

It is that last sentence, which I have italicized, that provides a ray of hope in the South African Christian *apartheid* dilemma. Christianity will ultimately climb out of its racial morass in South Africa, and elsewhere too, through its doctrine of the Church which either is the Body of Christ as the New Testament epistles describe it, or else a mockery of God and man which had better be abandoned.

Racism in Africa takes many forms such as general and particular phobias against 'the blacks', bias against African ways and culture, a paternal condescension, and an inner feeling of superiority on the part of whites. (Africans also, let it be said, are often racists in the reverse manner.) Within the Church racism is seen in its *apartheid* aspect—an organized and even understandable form of racism—but it is also seen in a tacit acceptance of the fact that in general Christianity appears as the white man's religion which he practises in different levels at different times, to the deep disillusionment of the African as he contemplates the process.

The situation may be looked at in this way. *First* there is the Christianity of the basic beliefs, the pure milk of the word, as the African hears it in school and as expounded in church. This is Biblical Christianity which the Christian advocate claims to be the basis of all his beliefs and practices. Then, *secondly* the African meets his first level of Christianity in the missionary, his family, and the mission group in general living usually in their spacious bungalows and inevitably separated from the African way of life. *Thirdly* comes the white man in administration, offices, stores and mines whose attitude is frequently a bold denial of what the African thinks Christianity is. *Fourthly,* if the African moves into the land of a so-called Christian nation he receives another series of shocks about Christianity, and is probably so affronted in his own personal dignity that he is disillusioned for ever about the Christian faith.

Out of all this comes the wide and misguided generalization that the white man is primarily a racist, and that his religion has little to do with his conduct or his relationships with other people. Mr Henry Makulu, Associate Director of the Ecumenical Institute, Bossey, reports a conversation with an African student. 'Christianity is a white man's weapon,' he was told. 'It is used to weaken the African, but now we have a new weapon to fight them; we have discovered politics!'

That all white men are not racists, and anti-black, is Africa's discovery in recent years and many of them have found their inspiration in the Christian religion and in the Christian Church. But the swift surge of African life in desiring to be known and recognized for what an African is in his own right, unequivocally, has often beclouded many well-meant enterprises of white origin. I think for instance of the fine ideals of the Capricorn Society with its vision of 'common citizenship', the idea of 'partnership', the genuine beliefs which lie behind words like 'multi-racial' and 'non-racial'—all of which have been besmirched in usage and have come to be regarded by Africans as mere subterfuges of the whites to maintain their supremacy.

What remains for positive good? The Church with all its faults still holds the gift of the good life for Africa, a Church which is neither black nor white but Christian without dot, comma or explanation. Nothing short of that will meet the needs of the new Africa.

Thirdly, Christianity is on its mettle in Africa as an opponent of *Communism.* Communism is not at the moment an immediate threat to any African country, nor is it a danger to the growth of the Christian Church, but by its very nature it is capable of springing surprises and of winning its battles from within the life of a people. It must be taken seriously in Africa. I remember travelling in the 'cocoa country' of Ghana and being greeted in the house of the local chief. On his desk were a number of leaflets about Communism sent to him by the United States Information Office in Accra. He viewed the gift with a mild humour remarking that if the United States had not told him about it he would never have heard of Communism!

There are said to be a number of favourable factors for the growth of Communism in the African countries such as: (*a*) the appeal of Communism as over against a dying colonialism; (*b*) the link between African communalism and what Communism may offer in politics and technology; (*c*) the neutrality of the new African nations, playing into the hands of the Soviet Union; (*d*) the possibility of a 'people's movement' in rebellion against the new nationalisms. In addition to the attention that the Soviet Union is giving to visits from African leaders, the large number of student-scholarships that are being offered to Africans in Soviet universities, and the practical aid in loans and technical assistance, are all part of the Communist infiltration plan.

Even more significant is the penetration of Africa by radio from Communist countries. According to an investigation by the BBC Monitoring Service (January 1961), the USSR devotes thirty-eight and a half hours every week in talks in English and French to Africa, and fifty hours in Arabic. From China come thirty-five hours in English and fourteen in Arabic, while Eastern Germany has forty-nine hours in Arabic. The Soviet satellite countries, Albania, Bulgaria, Czechoslovakia, Hungary and Roumania, add their quota of English, French, Portuguese, with the USSR including three and a half hours a week in Swahili.

Against the growth of Communism are seen factors like these: (*a*) the power of African nationalism, and its leadership which is still in full cry against any dependence on richer countries, including Russia; (*b*) the rural conservatism of Africa, based on a communal peasant economy that is not dominated by landlordism; (*c*) the African educated, governmental élite draw their democratic inspirations from the West; and (*d*) there is no sustained doctrinal study of Marxism in relation to the African situation.

Communism knows that the African revolution has only just begun, and that the 'hour of meaninglessness' which proclaims the emptiness of political nationalism, and the fatuity of all the hopes which nationalism has aroused, has not yet struck. Communism is waiting for the arrival of the vacuum in African life, when the rootless men, and the men of no religion, take charge and move in to power. Meanwhile it is co-operating wherever it can in undercutting ties with the West and in subversive acts to undermine the traditional links with Europe which include Christianity.

It is precisely the threatened vacuum that religion has to fill in Africa. Nasser is boldly claiming that Islam alone is capable of doing it and of dealing with Communism in Africa, and that Christianity offers little possibility of stemming the red tide once it begins to flow in Africa.

The shadow of Communism is a warning once again to Christianity that only an indigenous, missionary minded Church will be capable of meeting Africa's needs and of providing soul and substance for a people in revolution.

As the African countries move into power on their own so Communism is on the alert to exploit the international possibilities of local difficulties, as it did in the Congo only to be baulked by United Nations action. Communism, if it is to fulfil its global dreams, must find a footing in an Africa that is within the arena of the cold war, not simply as an appendage to Europe, but in its own right. The outburst of indignation at the use of the Sahara for the explosion of atomic bombs was an example of how Africa feels when it is still treated as a European 'dog's body'.

After a journey through Africa a London *Times* correspondent summed up his impressions, in relation to the Communist threat, as follows:

> Over and above the Congo, the Western world has to decide its attitude over three main issues in Africa. These are the future of the white minorities: the extent and method of applying economic aid: and defence . . . to arrive at right conclusions is easier when one is finally rid of certain prevalent illusions—the illusion that the cold war can be excluded from Africa: the illusion that African countries have no policy-making will of their own: the illusion that African interests can be horse-traded in matters which are primarily the interests of others.[1]

Communism will zealously foster all Europe's illusions about Africa while conducting its own brand of 'cold war' inside Africa with astute realism. It sees the experimentation of the African revolution swiftly mounting in ideas and inventions, a situation that is ideal for Communist penetration and persuasion and one that (with China in mind) should forewarn and forearm the Christian Church.

[1] *The Times*, 11.3.61.

5

HOW CHRISTIAN IS AFRICA?

THAT IS the central question of this book, and how to answer it is my main problem. No one has ever done an exact census of the numbers of Christians in Africa, and even if they had would that be the answer? How Christian is Britain? It is easy enough to quote the annual returns of the two great churches of these islands, the Churches of England and Scotland, and to say that is the answer however dismal it may be. For instance the Church of England reports that about twenty-seven millions of adult people are baptized members of it, about nine millions are confirmed, and less than three millions observe their basic commitment of membership which is usually stated as Communion on Easter Day. But is that a fair estimate of life in the Anglican Church?

Total figures for Christian Africa must probably bear the same kind of whittling down process, but the trouble is to settle what are the totals. Even such eminent Africanists as Dr Roland Oliver and Bishop Bengt Sundkler are separated by millions in their estimates. But both are agreed that the tenth parallel of North Latitude is the religious frontier of Africa, the line that runs from the Atlantic coast at Sierra Leone, and reaches the Indian Ocean in Somalia. South of that line is Africa South, the area of the continent where the Christian Church has some claim to be rooted and, at any rate, has something to show in great numbers for its hundred years of life—much less than that in many areas.

There are probably about 230 million black people in

the whole of the continent of whom some 75 millions live to the north of the religious frontier and, except for ten millions, are mainly Muslim. South of the frontier the 125 millions include over 52 million Christians. This last figure comes from the *World Christian Handbook* (1962), which surveys the growth of the Christian community in Africa South. The survey tells of the golden years of Christianity's advance in Africa. In 1900 the Christian community belonging to the Anglican and Protestant communities in Africa numbered 560,000. By 1957 it had leaped to 12,625,000. In 1962 it was 18,956,398.

Almost every conceivable Christian organization, denomination, mission and church has shared in this phenomenal growth, with some remarkable advances in the latter part of the period by the Pentecostalists and Seventh-Day Adventists who now number about a million of the Protestant total. The vigorous work of these groups gives point to an amusing (if it were not pathetic) letter received in July 1961 in a mission board office in London from a Ghana schoolmaster asking for help in writing a book. He finished up:

> You may be glad to learn that I am a retired First Class schoolmaster trained by the Basel Missionaries. I am also a Methodist, a Salvationist, a Seventh-Day Adventurist and an Apostolic in order to acquire the necessary knowledge befitting a matured Protestant.

Christianity is paying a heavy price for its advance in Africa!

But to complete the picture we must look at the most remarkable advance of all, that of the Roman Catholic Church which the Handbook estimates to have risen in Africa South from a community of 18 millions in 1957 to a total community of nearly 29 millions in 1962, thus completing the estimate of some 48 million Christians all told.

Rome was late on the scene in modern Africa. But a succession of famous missionary encyclicals in 1919, 1926 and 1957 laid down the Roman strategy in Africa which has paid off so handsomely. Backed by the dedicated power of the missionary orders—notably the White Fathers under their great founder and general, Cardinal Charles Lavigerie (1825-1892)—the Roman Church concentrated its strength in certain areas such as Uganda, Ruanda-Urundi, the Congo and Eastern Nigeria. In Urundi in 1922 there were only 14,500 baptized Roman Catholics with 15 European priests and no African priests. By 1957 the totals were 1,200,000, 244 and 117. In East Africa, as a whole, it is claimed that ten per cent of the population, or some three millions, belong to the Roman Catholic community with the greatest concentration (24 per cent) in Uganda and a million in Tanganyika, which can now boast the first African cardinal of modern times, Cardinal Laurian Rugambwa.

This swift rise of the Roman Catholic Church in Africa South is characterized by certain aspects of church strategy designed to make the Church thoroughly African in its theology and its philosophical outlook. The Roman Church evidently sees the possibility in Africa of recovering the sense of community which has been largely lost in the West, and its younger priests are encouraged 'to think black' in order to be in touch with the rising tide of African cultural thought. The movement of the 'lay apostolate', so noticeable everywhere in the Roman Church, is also growing in Africa following the impetus given to it in 1955 by the first Leaders' Meeting of the Lay Apostolate for Africa, in Uganda. Since the 1950s the consecration of African bishops has proceeded apace; some sixteen Africans are now bishops.

All Christian traditions in Africa have had their experience of 'mass movements', the influx of large numbers of people into the Christian Church with the many perils attached to it. Thirty years ago all the missions of the

Anglican, Methodist, Lutheran, Presbyterian and Baptist churches in West and East Africa and in Congo were reporting these movements which threatened to dislocate the life of the Church by what Roman Catholic observers call 'the law of strangulation' which stifles the genuine growth of the Church by its very numerical success.

Writing in 1924 the (then) Anglican Bishop of Lagos said:

> To baptize the hundreds who are flocking into the Church, unless we are prepared to continue their training and teaching, spells disaster in the future. In a district in which there were over 1,000 adult baptisms last year, there are over 200 congregations, and it takes at least five days to get from one end to the other. There is only one superintending missionary and four African clergy on the staff. . . . If the present opportunity is lost it will not recur. I do not fear that the growing African Church will be swept away; I am fearful as to the outstanding character it may assume in the future. What will be the general tone and level of the future Church?[1]

Lack of trained leadership in those years of bulk harvesting may well be one of the reasons for the sense of stagnation, and lack of vital directive which now pervades so many of those areas of one-time rapid growth. The intense conviction of the first-generation Christians has now given way to a visible deterioration in a third generation. It was with the generation in between that the real battle for Christian Africa was not decisively won.

But at the same time Christianity did dig for itself a firm rootage in Africa during these years, and its success cannot all be laid at the door of the white man and his powerful presence. Too often the kind of 'white man' who went to Africa as government officer, trader and business man in those vital years between 1900 and 1957 was non-Christian in his attitudes, or at least did not identify himself with

[1] Quoted in Sundkler's *Christian Ministry in Africa*, p. 69.

the missionary enterprise. He was a handicap rather than an asset to the growth of the faith. And yet Christianity triumphed in this numerically miraculous manner: there must be something in it that appeals to the African.

Christianity did not win its place in Africa merely because the white man recommended it. By its own appeal to Africans it showed itself to be a religion that met their needs and had close links with their own thought. It spoke of the Beginnings of Mankind, of the mysteries of Creation, of the Great Deity who embraced within his power the whole order of life divine and human. The Old Testament in particular is a very vital book in African Christianity with its stories of Creation and God's dealing with his People, and African preachers are adept at drawing parallels between their own traditional myths and the great Hebrew stories of the Old Testament.

As a Book of Remembrance the Old Testament reached back into the past of ancestors and linked the dead with the living. Genesis then becomes a living reality because the African Christian feels himself part of those things in the beginning and with the flesh and blood of living people who know God through the Community of God.

The Church comes naturally to the African. He must belong. He is part of the Tree of Life which extends its branches through time to eternity, and he finds the symbols and imagery which describe the Church very agreeable and very proper for a religion which is believed and practised in a fellowship. Many of the triumphant notes of the Christian faith which celebrate the Communion of the Saints and the Final Reign of God find fervent echoes in the African heart.

The Church as the Great Family, the Great Clan, which is all-inclusive of the living and the dead, and provides a place for everyone, is central to African Christian experience, and attempts which have been made to present the

Church as the Great Tribe, with Christ as its Great Chief, are along the line of African experience and understanding.

This view of the Church is the African setting for the Drama of Redemption, the advent of the Son of God into the human clan where He moves as the Second Adam to the fight and to the final victory. Bishop Sundkler quotes a Zulu preacher's sermon to show the depth and wonder of this conception:

> Consider that incredible joy, that indescribable jubilation which filled Adam's heart on the First Easter Morning as the Hero of Heaven came in through the Gate of Heaven, with His Crown of Thorns, now a brilliant Crown of Victory, walking the central aisle in the heavenly Temple, straight up to the Throne of the Almighty. There He gave His report that from this day Satan and Sin and Death had been overcome. For now He, the Second Adam, had won the victory (p. 284).

As Bishop Sundkler remarks, 'Here is a width of vision that takes in the whole history of Redemption and displays the whole drama of the Bible, from the Beginning to the consummation; this living African theology, born in the art of preaching. It is significant that it is the great Day of the Church's year, Easter Day, which calls out a message of this magnitude.'

Much of this magnificently positive theology in African Christianity has yet to be worked out by African theologians, and the full splendour of it may—as the Roman Church evidently believes—recover something of the lost radiance of the Christian faith. But there is a long way to go before the Church in Africa rises to the full height of its theological stature and moves out of its rut of legalism. Caught between the grip of the Bantu fertility cults which hold the African to his duty to his family, and the grip of the Christian religion, the Church turns to a harsh legalism in dealing with human nature. Ninety per cent of all cases of church discipline are concerned with sexual problems which for the non-Christian African are not—as in the West—held to be a serious lapse in moral standards but are a recognition of fertility as a social duty. The Great Commandment within the Church has become the one which forbids adultery, and the Church is so often reduced to a community of legalists ready to pronounce judgment.

Its liking for legalism is not to be despised, provided it is seen to be a preparation for the full Gospel of freedom in Christ. To be authoritarian in its attitude has been a necessary stage in the growth of African Christianity, for without it the sweep of Christian expansion in the last fifty years would have lost its momentum. The immense task of Christianizing the Church in its theology and practice will be the burden of Christianity's next fifty years in Africa.

Alongside legalism, *disunity* is a heavy handicap to Christianity in Africa. A man is a Roman Catholic, an Anglican, a Baptist, a Methodist or a Presbyterian chiefly through the chances of birth and geography, and rarely by choice. If it is Kenya you live in then the chances are you will be an Anglican (40,000), or a Presbyterian (25,000). In the north of Kenya you could be a Quaker (20,000), a member of what is said to be the largest Yearly Meeting of Friends in the world, mainly due to the work of the American Friends. But the Pentecostalists, the Seventh-Day Adventists and the Church of God can also produce 45,000 members, and the inter-denominational missions, such as the Africa Inland, another 10,000. Over the border in Tanganyika if you are not a Roman Catholic you would probably be a Lutheran (100,000) or an Anglican (80,000), and in Central Tanganyika most likely a Moravian (20,000). In Uganda the choice is pretty equal between Roman Catholics and the Anglican Church.

Swinging over to the west coast, Nigeria offers an astonishing choice of Christian allegiance with the Roman Catholics growing powerful in the east and the Anglicans

(100,000) and the Methodists (40,000) in the west. But you might also be a Baptist (30,000), an Evangelical Qua Iboe River Mission (44,000), a Presbyterian (15,000), a Lutheran (38,000), and, if in the north of Nigeria, almost certainly your Christianity would spring from one of the great non-denominational missions (15,000). In Ghana you probably would be either a Presbyterian (53,000) or a Methodist (50,000), and in the countries which once formed part of French West Africa, a Roman Catholic, a Reformed Church of France (12,000) or a Methodist (10,000).

In Congo the land is large enough to have a fantastic tapestry of churches, sects and missions which conform loosely to the word 'Protestant' and have a community of about a million people with the Baptists, Presbyterians and Disciples counting a membership of 80,000 each, the Adventists (20,000) and many other groups ranging from Assemblies of God, Free Methodists, Mennonites, and Independent Baptists to the labels Interdenominational and just Independent. In Angola, dominated like Congo by the Roman Catholic Church, Methodists number 30,000, the Church of Christ 30,000 and the Baptists 6,000.

Southwards the pattern of Protestant Christianity in the Rhodesias again provides a Christian kaleidoscope, except that in Northern Rhodesia the Presbyterian and Congregational Churches are now linked with those of Nyasaland in the Church of Central Africa with over 150,000 members preponderantly Presbyterian in Nyasaland. The Anglican diocese of Northern Rhodesia is small with 8,000 members; the Reformed Churches (largely directed from the Republic of South Africa) have 15,000, the Methodist 1,500, Baptists 2,000 and the Adventists 5,000. Southern Rhodesia has a similar pattern—Anglicans (25,000), Methodist (15,000), Reformed (5,000), Church of Central Africa (5,000), Adventists (15,000) and an abundant sprinkling of other churches and missions.

In the South African Republic black Christianity is

made to feel its sharp separateness from the rest of the Church even in those Christian communities where religious *apartheid* is not the official policy. But even the Dutch Reformed Churches, most rigid of all in race separation, direct a vigorous missionary work amongst Africans and have 100,000 members in their non-white churches. The other main groups are United Evangelical Lutheran (250,000), Anglican (200,000), Methodist (250,000), United Church or Congregational (70,000), and then follows an extraordinary multiform mixture of groups and sects with over a million members in the African separatist churches about which more will be said in the next chapter.

How Christian, then, is the Church in Africa? Here is another of those massive questions which have no final or even satisfactory answer. We can only take a few depth soundings, and one of them must be about *the pastor*.

Bishop Sundkler in his book *The Christian Ministry in Africa* describes some of the three hundred essays he secured from secondary school children in all parts of Africa on the subject, 'The Pastor in our Local Church'. He was surprised at the amount these children knew about the pastor and his work. 'Generally speaking,' he says,

> the school-age generation appear to appreciate the work of the pastor—although we shall probably do well to discard some of the most enthusiastic expressions of praise. They have discovered the fundamental role which the pastor plays as a social and religious leader in the local community. The historical perspective in which a Ghana Presbyterian schoolboy sees the arrival of the pastor is conceived in terms which we regard as memorable: 'It was one Sunday morning when the church room was crowded with people. Our catechist introduced the Pastor who had been commissioned to take charge of the Church in my area. *That was the first time in history.*' He was right, of course. The arrival of that pas-

tor did mean, perhaps to an even greater extent than the schoolboy had perceived, a new chapter in the local history of that church (p. 130).

But is there a genuinely Christian conception of 'the pastor' in Africa? The pattern largely imitates the West with the African pastor attempting to be the omnibus person that the Western missionary was often forced to be as a combination of administrator, school inspector, accountant, architect, preacher and pastor. Sometimes a particular 'mission' emphasized one aspect of the ministry, sacramental, teaching, industrial or rural uplift, and that too comes out in the African pastor. You can quickly distinguish between a Lutheran and an Adventist African pastor, and it must be admitted that as a consequence of the variety of missions and their methods there is no one Christian pattern of the pastor in Africa. But Bishop Sundkler sees emerging, even in the most extreme Protestant churches, 'a greater awareness of the place in the life of the Church of the ministry of the sacraments'. This, he thinks, will elevate the position of the pastor as the 'mid-man' between God and the people.

In illustration of this, Bishop Sundkler quotes a case of church discipline in the Lake Victoria area. A church elder had used the altar vessels for the brewing of beer. His fellow elders in the church council failed to convict him of his sin. He replied, 'You have no authority over me. I am just as good as you are.' Then the pastor began to speak:

> Now I am going to say my words, as a priest and as a man of God. Yes, of course you were right in doing what you did. Of course you were right in using the sacred vessels of the church for this unholy purpose. Of course you were right in carrying on like this. You will end by harvesting what you have sown, that which must be the obvious outcome of this, on the last Day before the

> Throne of Almighty God. You yourself have chosen. Carry on! Nobody will hinder you any longer (p. 305).

The misdoer was overcome by fright, and was reduced to tears and asked for forgiveness. Bishop Sundkler comments, 'In that congregation the pastor had established himself as something more than a mere group leader. Here was a priest of God, backed by the sanctions of the Holy Church, wielding the sword of the Spirit.'

The 'mid-man' in Africa, as elsewhere, can easily become a little boss, relying on his clerical position for his authority, and in Africa this danger is sharpened by the huge parishes with scattered congregations that he is expected to supervise. The tendency towards clericalism is partly a reflection of the patriarchalism of the Western missionary of an earlier generation, and the often prevailing view in Africa that promotion to ordination is a reward for long services to the Church, with the wearing of the clerical collar as an insignia of the honour achieved.

All this raises deep and vital questions for the Christian ministry in Africa which are the subject of an endless flow of views, investigations, reports and commissions. The judgment that is emerging is that African Christianity needs a two-stream ministry, one which has an educational and theological background, and a second that is also fully ordained but is based on the 'village catechist' or perhaps a 'voluntary ministry' of laymen.

How Christian is the *worship* of the Church in Africa? As we have already pointed out, the African Christian has an immediate understanding of the Church as an organic and corporate fellowship. He likes to express all this in his worship, which in song, rhythm and movement is often far removed from the more intellectual approach of Western Christianity. Choirs and singing are important, and the great festivals of the Christian year, with their climax at

Easter, can be the occasion of a three or four days' assembly for worship.

The African sense of the sacredness of 'table fellowship' is expressed in the observance of the Eucharist, and in the link the African sees between eating, drinking, prayer and song. It is in this sense that African Christianity is becoming perhaps more 'Christian' in its worship than the West because it emphasizes the wholeness of God's people, the family sense of 'belonging' to the total *laos* which is being partially experienced in the West through the growing emphasis on 'parish communion'. The Church in Africa has a special responsibility for the recovery of the whole *laos*: its sense of 'group fellowship' is strong, and its Christian heritage in the line of salvation history proceeding through the Old and the New Testaments is deep and abiding. The West has divided this wholeness into laity and clergy. Africa could recover this essential Christian unity by its worship and its gathering of the whole people of God.

Archbishop Temple used to say that 'when our worship is at its best our feelings are deeply stirred'—an experience which in Africa obviously calls for the Africanization of worship. But how is this to be done? What elements must be changed? At the All-Africa Conference at Ibadan in 1958, J. H. Nketia of University College, Ghana, pointed out the difference between 'indigenous worship' and 'Christian worship' is that 'Christ is a historical fact'. He is not an 'ancestor', not 'a man in the world of the dead'. but the risen Lord. Mr Nketia pointed out that for worship in Africa to be Christian two aspects of worship must be retained. One is the traditional observances of Christian worship which give it universality, and the other is the Reformation principle of bringing the faith home to ordinary people in the language they understand. He says: 'the purpose of Africanization is not the abandonment of Christocentric worship but the use of familiar means of expression to enable the African worshipper to understand better and feel more deeply. It should make use of techniques of worship already developed in Africa consistent with the quality and purpose of Christian worship'.

So the question for Africa is not only 'Is the worship Christian?' but 'Is the worship African too?' The idiom and style of African Bible translations and of various church liturgies are not yet adequate, 'We must await Africans endowed both with deep Christian conviction and with perfect knowledge of our languages' says J. H. Nketia, 'to re-create worship in a truly African idiom'. This is particularly true in music. Western hymns are still Western in their poetry, and imported Western tunes lack an appeal to Africa where words and melody go together. 'The Western tune often turns the whole thing upside down. What is more, the tune may even convey the wrong meaning because of wrong intonation.' J. H. Nketia makes an appeal for the poetic use of the drum in African worship. At appropriate moments it can help the African as he tries to concentrate all his faculties on Christ in public worship.[1]

How Christian is Africa in regard to *the Bible*? One central clue to the Bible appears to have emerged into African church life, and that is the belief that the Bible is about the People of God in history, and that the continuity from Abraham through the Old Testament to the People of Christ in the New Testament and the Church today is the heart of its meaning. This is most thoroughly Christian and most thoroughly African too.

But all observers of the church in Africa comment on the excessive interest in the Old Testament. The International Missionary Council's 1954 survey of the ministry in Africa declared:

> The Old Testament offers to the African student unusual attractions in its narratives, its concrete character and its

[1] *The Church in Changing Africa*, pp. 59-65.

powerful imagery. The historical books provide a philosophy, an explanation for the origins of the universe and of man. There is also the fascination of the proverbs, with their moralizing application to daily life and the interest of comparison with African folk wisdom. The description of Hebrew customs, the sacrifices, the legal provisions, entrance many students in the resemblances to elements of African life. Here are excellent points of contact for greater teachers. Here are also perils for lesser teachers. Preoccupation with the historical and legal books sometimes cheats the Psalms and the Prophets of their rightful portion. Moreover the time and interest expended on the Old Testament may leave inadequate place for the New (p. 60).

This excessive interest in the Old Testament leads to legalism in African church life which can only be eradicated by the view of the New Testament as the fulfilment of the Old in the Person of Jesus Christ. Another way is for pastors and preachers to study, discuss and expound the great Biblical words, 'tracing their meaning through the Old and the New Testament and noting how the essential beliefs of the Christian hinge upon these basic conceptions. Such word-studies would be studies in that "Communication" which is more than translation.'[1]

Africa has the complete Bible in only 57 of its hundreds of languages. Its pastors and preachers have to use translations which are often out-dated, and they need to be competent in French, English or Portuguese in order to elucidate the meaning of the Scriptures. Portions of the Scriptures, usually a Gospel and the Psalms, are available in 180 languages. We are asking a mighty question when we pose the proposition about Africa's Christian use of the Bible. It could properly be claimed that she has not yet had a fair chance of showing what she can do.

It is the same with that other tool of the faith—*Christian*

[1] IMC Report, Part 3 (1954), pp. 45-6.

literature. Late in the field and still in the pioneer stages of production, Christian literature in Africa is handicapped by a multiplicity of languages, the lack of a comprehensive strategy, the poor supply of authors and the difficulties of distribution. But the widening area of educated people, and the attack on illiteracy by both government and voluntary agencies, have compelled the Church to sharpen this powerful tool and to use it more effectively.

It might well be asked, 'How Christian is Christian literature?' The answer is largely conditioned by Africa's demand for books covering the whole range of reading. The bookshops of such agencies as the United Society for Christian Literature and the Society for Promoting Christian Knowledge are in Africa homes of 'good books', places where the African reader is able to browse. In that sense 'Christian literature' is as wide as may be. But it also has its specific meaning in such series as *World Christian Books* and *Key Books*. Started in 1955 under the editorship of Bishop Stephen Neill, *World Christian Books* has now 48 titles in its list, all of them strictly attuned to serving the Christian faith and first of all published in English. It has now 35 translations in some of the major Asian languages including Japanese, Chinese, Tamil, Telegu and Arabic. But African languages lag behind. At the moment of writing in mid-1962 only four African languages have copies of *World Christian Books* translated.

There are reasons for this African lag: the dominance of English amongst Christians able to read and profit from these books, the small areas served by some of the African languages, and the meagre market amongst Christians. Undoubtedly Africa is growingly book-conscious, and there is evidence that 'books' do not only mean 'text-books' for examination purposes. What the Church has to do is to nurse a market of readers who will want to venture beyond the necessities of examinations, and to read intelligently about the Christian faith as a whole.

'Christian literature' is an evangelistic instrument of immense potentiality. It must include all sorts of 'literature' in its armoury if it is to be a genuine Christian tutor for life and how to live it. Africa has already shown in a series of notable Christian journals such as *Envol, Africa Challenge, New Day* and *Rock* that there is a readership and a response for the printed page, and that response is likely to mount as Africa abolishes illiteracy and becomes a continent of readers.

6

DANGERS AND DILEMMAS

I ONCE heard a missionary with many years of distinguished service in East Africa say that he had never seen a lion in Africa. The news ought not to have surprised me. He kept his eye open for people. That was his Africa. Yours may be the Africa of wild life, the last unalloyed arena of the world's great beasts, or it may be the Africa of mines and investments where the entrepreneur manoeuvres amongst the continent's raw materials. You may—and quite rightly—be romantic about Africa, about its history, geography and particularly its missionary story.

Every man has his own Africa, and there are dangers lurking in every conception of this hard and earthy continent. For the Christian man it is difficult to get a comprehensive Christian view of the continent. You see a bit of Anglican Africa, or a Lutheran Africa, or a Roman Catholic Africa. There lies one of the major dangers for the future of the Christian faith in Africa. *Can it become a Christian continent without a united Christian Church?*

I need not rehearse the story of the Christian scramble for Africa in the last century, which portrayed both the glory and the misery of the Christian Church and provided the impetus for so much that Africa needed. If the Christian Church could have its time over again in Africa I am convinced that it would organize itself differently and have a plan of action from the start. But even so, granted the historic Western separations of the Church, it might still mean an Anglican bloc in East Africa and a Methodist bloc in West Africa and so on. Africa is big enough to carry even the imported disunities of the Church, and in practice the urge towards unity in recent years in Africa has nearly always come from the white man. It is he who has been sensitive about the divisions of the Church and has instigated most of the movements towards unity. He has had a guilt complex about the proliferation of the imported sects. Africans have been on the whole rather passive, wondering why it takes so long for union to come about and believing that the non-African factors in the process are responsible for the delays as well as for the initiatives.

We have sadly to admit that a new religious scramble for Africa has taken place since the second world war. It might be called the scramble of the sects, and the independent mission organizations which have not always been ready to observe the agreed lines of demarcation between the older established missions and churches. Armed with considerable resources, usually from North America, the independent groups have appeared to be more mobile, more filled with the zeal of evangelism than other groups and their outreach into the African pagan world has provided their missions with an aggressive renown. They have in many places also secured a following recruited from the ranks of the organized churches which has only added to the bewilderment of the African.

'To whom shall he go?' The Rev. R. K. Macdonald asked this question at the All-African Conference at Ibadan in 1958:

> He sees the piety of the Muslims, the strict discipline of the Roman Catholic, and he knows many keen and enthusiastic Anglicans, Methodists, Presbyterians, Baptists, Congregationalists, Brethren, Seventh-day Adventists and Jehovah's Witnesses. Church history means nothing to him. To whom shall he go? With all this bewildering competition will he not prefer the unity of the Muslim faith to the divided Christ? Every reunion of our divided ranks makes the call of Christ clearer to him. . . . Dare

we continue to let him hear a confused mumble when we presume to call ourselves heralds of Christ?

But there is even a deeper question than the disunity of the organized Christian Church, and that is the question of how to let the Church become African. For a hundred years and more the planting of Christianity, its direction and its policy making, have been largely conducted from outside Africa. It has been far easier to discover what is going on in Christian affairs in Africa in London, New York, Basel and Toronto than in Accra, Nairobi, Salisbury and Johannesburg. Africa, as far as Christianity is concerned, has been an appendage of Europe and North America. Except for the Republic of South Africa, nominal independence in church life has been geared to a European pattern in worship, leadership, finance and ideas. In effect Christianity in Africa South owes its life largely to non-African parents, and the mark of its heredity is strongly upon it.

The 'missionary culture' of African Christianity is all-pervasive although individual missionaries have done their utmost, particularly in the last ten years, by self-denying ordinances, of every description, to step out of the role of leadership and to dispel the idea that the church belonged to them. I remember the despair with which a CMS missionary viewed a notice board on the road to Onitsha in Eastern Nigeria which loudly proclaimed 'CMS Mission', and in small lettering 'Diocese of the Niger'. The letters 'CMS' carried a kind of nostalgic-magic which was almost impossible to eradicate. They had passed into the world of legend and memory for the African, and it was he who refused to abandon them.

This affection for a noble memory is a likeable enough trait amongst many African Christians of the older generations who themselves have imbibed some of the 'missionary culture', and indeed owe their own life and livelihood to it.

What do the younger ones think? They are more likely to agree with the appraisal of F. B. Welbourn, who with the experience of Uganda in mind says:

> Missionaries have taken to Africa a complex culture which it is perhaps easiest to call 'Christian-western', in which the faith is extricably inter-woven with the techniques and values of a civilization which it has itself helped to create.
>
> It is necessary to insist on this close identity, in African eyes, of all Christian missionaries with Western political power and material culture, because, while missionaries were themselves divided into distinct theological, and perhaps national, groups . . . missionaries are Europeans, offering a culture which is Western as well as Christian, unable to escape—whether they wish it or not—from identification with men of other professions but the same race.[1]

Africans respond (according to Mr Welbourn) 'out of their total culture to men who, whatever their intentions, are seen as closely identified with the whole culture of the west and, despite the predominantly Christian emphasis of the presentation, share with their compatriots many attitudes which are not necessarily Christian in origin and may, indeed, belong essentially to the "British" or "French" or "American" rather than to the "Christian" *schema*'.

In other words, Africa has yet fully to respond to Christianity. Its response so far has been to a mixture of 'Christian-Western' Christianity now heavily institutionalized after the Western pattern with Africans doing things in European style and becoming fossilized in the process. To claim that an African Archdeacon is not fully equipped for his office unless rigged out in his Anglican uniform, treasuring a Book of Common Prayer translated in an incomprehensible fashion from sixteenth-century English,

[1] *East African Rebels*, pp. 170 ff.

are examples of the 'Christian-Western' culture from which African Christianity must be liberated.

We now see many of the mistakes of the 'missionary past' in Africa, but it is most unlikely that Westerners will be the liberators of African Christianity. That liberation will proceed from Africans themselves who look at Christianity through their own eyes.

Meanwhile, *the 'independent' or 'separatist' churches* pose the question of Africanization in a spectacular way. Christened with variegated sets of names, they are to be found in most parts of the continent. In the Republic of South Africa alone, the government has registered some 2,000 of them.

Many reasons have been put forward for the existence and multiplication of these 'independent' groups, some of which are strictly orthodox in their Christian beliefs, although others come near to being outcrops of pagan cults. Their story makes fascinating reading,[1] and their existence suggests that Christianity has yet to discover the clue to the religious heart of Africa, for all these 'independent' groups are spontaneously African. Racialism, nationalism, pan-Africanism, polygamy, rebellion against ordered society and a struggle against the impersonal, large-scale, life which threatens to engulf the African in the town; these are all to be found amongst the reasons for this outburst of religious 'independence'. But Bishop Sundkler and Mr Welbourn in their books suggest that the real reason goes deeper—to an urge on the part of the African to have some place, amidst the accumulating debris of African life, where he can *feel at home*, where he can recognize his fellow men face to face, salute them as his brethren, and

[1] See *Bantu Prophets in South Africa* by Bengt Sundkler (1st ed. Lutterworth Press; 2nd ed. Oxford Press); *East African Rebels* by F. B. Welbourn (SCM Press); *Black Woman In Search of God* by Mia Brandel-Syrier (Lutterworth Press); and *Prophetism in Ghana* by C. G. Baëta (SCM Press).

have an identity himself. He wants to belong to a fellowship where his whole personality is at home, and where the Western Christian's distinction between 'religion' and 'ordinary life' is, at least momentarily, abolished.

In her remarkable study of the women's *manyanos* (meaning 'to join' or 'unite') in South Africa, Mrs Brandel-Syrier says that 'European Christianity has been brought to the African as an ideal construct of the highest minds, a luminous cloud floating high above the baser, everyday, concrete things of life. No wonder the African people are increasingly forming their own Christian Churches in which God is again *in* the scheme of things.'

She describes life inside the *manyanos,* which, although connected mainly with the chief religious denominations, are powerfully independent with a kind of 'tribal' life of their own in which loyalty, discipline, generosity are expected of the members. 'The desire to be left alone to do things themselves, in their own way,' she says, 'is growing amongst Africans in general, men and women. . . . They have learned by experience that European assistance, however well-intentioned, has crushed their self-expression and smothered their sense of responsibility. So they "make their own laws for themselves" and push the Europeans out.'

Education, civilization, and the technical 'know-how' of modern man have gone along with Christianity in Africa and we have assumed that this is the Christianizing mission of the church. But the 'independent' churches speak for something deeper in worship, ritual and a sense of the eternal. In fact they are part of modern Africa's search for God, and instead of being amongst 'the dangers' to Christianity they may well be pointers to the renewal of the Church's whole life.

Two other 'dangers' for the life of Christianity in Africa may be briefly mentioned. One is *the cold war,* which is using Africa as its latest battleground, and the other a threat to 'religious freedom' of which there are signs in various parts.

I have already in chapter 4 indicated some of the threats to Christianity in Africa which could arise from the planting of an indigenous Communism. But the 'cold war' is an attempt to break through the neutralism of the new African countries with the offer of aid in cash and kind (Russian snow-ploughs have been sent to Guinea!), and to keep alive all the resentful memories of colonialism that linger in African hearts and minds. Christianity can so easily be amongst the 'resentful memories' associated with past colonial regimes unless it has a vigorous indigenous of its own which is seen to be truly African.

China in particular is able to make an appeal in Africa by suggesting that conditions in Africa are very similar to those which prevailed in China immediately prior to the revolution. She is anxious to pose as the leader against world imperialism, and is ready to back all forms of African political extremism whether nationalistic or Communist-inspired. Nothing could be more apt for this purpose than a drive against Christianity as the running dog of the Western imperialists. Again the life of Christianity on this 'cold-war' front depends on its African vitality.

Threats to *religious liberty* have been prevalent in Africa all through the years of Christianity's expansion. They have taken various forms. In Northern Nigeria the British government in its day prevented missions from spreading in a Muslim territory, and in Angola and Mozambique the Portuguese government have never been happy with Protestant missions.

There are now signs that the new African nationalisms, too, are not free from this bug. The most recent case is the dismissal from Northern Nigeria of the Dutch Reformed Mission of South Africa after fifty years of devoted work amongst the Tiv people. No doubt hatred of the *apartheid* doctrine of South Africa is at the root of the decision. But nevertheless it is a threat to freedom of movement and access which are part of the whole concept of religious liberty which Christianity believes is the heritage of all free men and the right of all religions. As authoritarian government grows in Africa this previous right may well be in danger. It will be a test for African Christianity to measure its belief in liberty over against the power of states which like 'strong' government.

Nationalism is both a 'danger' and a 'dilemma' for the Christian Church in Africa. It has come upon her with an upsurge of emotion and passion that is bound to produce excesses of zeal, and the threat to religious freedom is only one of the dangers.

The dilemmas are much more subtle. How should the Church act in a country moving on to independence, or newly arrived at the goal? 'We have our flag, our motto and our national anthem,' said a delegate from Cameroun at the All-Africa Ibadan Conference 1958, and then went on to say 'that the church authorities are so passive in the face of such a tense situation'. What he meant was that the Church appeared to be indifferent to Cameroun's newly achieved status, and was not on the march with the politicians and the nation-makers. He recognized the Church's dilemma in these words:

> The minister is at the head of the Church; he is also a citizen of the country. He cannot and must not be ignorant of what is happening in his country. What is difficult or dangerous for him is that he has, in his parish, people of all opinions. It is his duty to know the opinion of each one and to lead him back to the right way if he goes wrong. He must have eyes to see, ears to hear, and he must be wise in what he says. In no circumstances can he bring politics or party spirit into his sermons, for that

would impede his ministry and make his work impossible.[1]

At the same conference Mr Alan Paton said some wise words about the attitude of the Church and the Christian towards the State. He pointed out the place of the two orders of society, the temporal and the spiritual, and of the duty of the Church to assist the State in maintaining and perhaps even recognizing those supratemporal foundations on which the good society is founded. And Christians, far from removing themselves from the world, have a duty towards it.

But he feared that the churches in Africa had not really faced up to their duty towards the State because of their misconception of what was political and what was not. Looking at Africa from the standpoint of his own South Africa, Mr Paton said:

> Our churches are to a dangerous degree conforming churches, and instead of transforming society, have become conformed to it. . . . In racial matters the South African churches obey the customs of the country rather than the great commandments. Many of them, indeed, have persuaded themselves that the customs of the country in racial matters are a direct consequence of obedience to the great commandments. This conformity goes to great lengths. . . . Of course the Church has a conserving function, but its duty is not to preserve the *status quo*; its duty is to conserve those supra-temporal foundations on which the *status quo* was based. The people of Africa are on the march into the modern age; and the Church must march with them, the guardian not of what is old but of what is ageless.[2]

The Church in Africa as the guardian of 'justice, love and truth' and as a tutor in freedom to the newly independent states—that is an arduous role for groups of Christians

[1] *The Church in Changing Africa*, p. 48. [2] p. 54.

barely equipped themselves in an understanding of the Church's duty within a modern state. It is perhaps asking too much of churches which have rarely reached maturity, and find themselves trapped in the dilemma of what is 'politics' and what is 'religious', a distinction which in the societies and tribes of the old Africa did not arise. The West has imposed on Africa part of its own dilemma, and must not be disappointed if Africa too is unsure about the answers.

But at the same time it will be no service to the African Church and African Christians to suggest that they should burke the issues. Alan Paton says:

> The task of asserting spiritual authority in a rapidly changing society and of rebuking excesses of nationalism after an era of subordination will not be easy. But it will be made easier if the Church manifests in itself the kind of society that it longs to see in the body politic.

The developing nationalisms in Africa are bound to confront the Church in the next decade with political and religious issues which will largely decide what sort of Christianity Africa is to have—a strong virile, independent Church, or one which conforms to the State and is content to live its life to itself in a kind of Christian ghetto. If it can climb out of its dilemma in relationship to the State the Church will be of immense influence in guiding the new Africa. For, as Alan Paton said at the Ibadan Conference:

> The power to govern is a heady wine, especially for those who have not tasted it before. There will be a great temptation to over-govern, to take unprecedented powers to do unprecedented tasks and to diminish the area of personal freedom. If Russian influence increases on this continent, and it seems likely to do, there will be a tendency for states to take more and more powers, whether under Russian influence or in opposition to it, and a temptation to hasten progress so that the world may see

> how much more advanced we might have been, had history not been so unkind to us (p. 55).

Another dilemma which the Church carries with it in Africa is a new view of 'the missionary' and of his place in the Church and in African life. To African nationalists eager to throw off every vestige of dependence on white interests and white control 'the missionary' appears to be a representative of the colonial past. There are many in the Church who share this view, and yet also see 'the missionary' as a colleague in the life of the Church who is still valued for his own sake and for the service he can render to the developing Church.

At the New Delhi Assembly of the World Council of Churches on 23 November 1961, Sir Francis Ibiam made these points in a notable speech:

> The Churches in Africa still need missionaries, and will continue to welcome them cordially for many years to come. They must however be men and women who will be prepared to work alongside the African on equal terms of partnership and mutual respect. The responsible African is anxious to get at grips with high responsibility and to play his or her part nobly in the affairs of the Church of his own community, and indeed in the affairs of the ecumenical movement. He must be given a chance. The avowed and dedicated African, I believe, constitutes the best investment in the dissemination of the Word of God amongst his fellow Africans. The right type of African Christian is not lacking in these days. . . . The good missionary must be on the look-out for such a one.

Sir Francis went on to suggest some of the conditions for missionary service as he saw it:

> If a missionary *believes* in human rights and privileges and that in every human society and environment every man has every right to attain to the highest possible development of which man is capable; if the missionary *believes* that all men are equal in the sight of God; if

the missionary *believes* that the African, like any other human being, has his own prestige, and his own peculiar, but nevertheless cherished, tradition, and yet the missionary respects it even though this might not conform to *his* own particular tradition; then I personally do believe and I am definitely certain that his tours in Africa, for long or short, would be very happy and his services would help to knit together in one bond of Christian fellowship the people of his homeland and Africa.

The dilemma of the Western missionary in Africa, as well as elsewhere in the traditional 'mission fields' of the world, will continue to be a sharp one especially in those areas where the Church is in a strongly nationalist atmosphere. No amount of theorizing by Western missionary-theologians about the unique ecumenical and representative character of 'the missionary' is likely to help solve the dilemma. What will help is the practical experience of churches in Asia and Africa in responding to the mission of the Church by sending forth missionaries themselves. This is already happening in Asia. Meanwhile 'the missionary' will continue to find himself frustrated, suspected and even opposed in his service to the Church. He must count this as part of the discipline of his calling.

An example of this opposition occurred in August 1962 when the Bishop of Accra, the Rt. Rev. Richard Roseveare, was expelled from Ghana on account of his criticism of the 'godless' atmosphere of Ghana's youth organization, the Young Pioneers. Bishop Roseveare believed that it was his duty to speak in the name of Christianity and the Church on the dangers of training youth in an 'atheistic' manner, a protest which was supported by the Presbyterian and Methodist Churches. This might be the beginning of a conflict between Church and State, and also a signal that African countries will not be exempt from a struggle which, in both East and West, Christianity has had to face.

7

SOME DISCOVERIES

ENOUGH OF dangers and dilemmas! Let us turn more cheerfully to some of the *discoveries* in faith which Africa provides. Too often Africa is thought of as a vast receiving receptacle, always accepting but rarely offering gifts to the whole Church. It certainly looks like that—and, whatever changes may come in the years ahead in political, economic and church life, Africa will always be a receiving land. The world's debt to Africa can never be adequately met. She has a permanent overdraft on the Christian conscience, a debt of honour that calls for copious supplies of service and dedication from the rest of the Church.

But Africa will also contribute to the life of the Church—and will make its gift in its own way. I remember standing one day in the Anglican cathedral at Onitsha in Eastern Nigeria and getting a vision of Africa's offering to the Christian faith. The great church slowly rising above the Niger has a fascinating array of coloured glass, long windows so arranged as to deflect the direct rays of the sun. All round the altar the sun of Africa glows in multi-form glory, not in one sheet of golden light but in an assembly of wonder. The invading sun appears to beckon all the varieties of Africa's life to the Holy Table with no one of them dominant, but all glowing and growing round the Table in a continuous co-operative glitter.

I think that the clue to African Christianity lies somewhere in this glowing iridescence. The Western, individualistic conception of Christianity hopes and expects to see emerge in African life great theologians, profound writers, great bishops and wise statesmen. It tends to be disappointed when the great ones do not appear. All sorts of excuses are made for their non-appearance in the Western style of greatness. It may be that one of the surprises of African Christianity in store for the whole church is its conception of another kind of greatness, the greatness of the whole church, a glowing, tumultuous whole dependent not on a few outstanding personalities but on the rich quality and variety of the total company.

Africa is now creating her own personality. She is doing so politically, and—very slowly—ecclesiastically. The 'independent' congregations and women's organizations already commented on are examples of the 'Africanism' of the Church and the personality it is now acquiring. It looks as if African Christianity will move away from its copying and aping Western forms of the Christian faith in worship and observances, and strike out in ways that may be unfamiliar and even grotesque to the West but truly African for the African.

Much attention is being paid to the revision of the Bible in African languages and in providing new portions of Scripture as well as complete Bibles in the vernaculars as they are used now. The same process needs to be applied to hymn-books. In his study of *African Music and the Church in Africa,* Henry Weman says:

> African hymn writing is called for; this art must develop freely according to its own rules, inspired by its own imagery and its own thought-world. . . . Any new African hymn book must be created by Africans, and it is the first task of the leaders of the churches to provide the inspiration to this end. This ought to be possible without any admixture of Western influence, as the growth of African art has demonstrated (p. 206).

Mr Weman also makes a plea for the use of African music in the life of the Church, pointing out that whereas in the West music is considered to be an expression of art providing edification, enjoyment and relaxation for the listeners, in Africa music-making is the concern of everyone. 'It is uncommon for the African to play *for* someone; he would rather play *with* someone. In popular music-making there are seldom passive listeners. The solo singer draws a spontaneous reaction from those who stand around, all take part in what is going on' (p. 20). It is the co-operative glow of colour and warmth round the Holy Table that Africa seeks, rather than the brilliant individual performance.

This view of African Christianity may also offer a clue to a deeper understanding of the place of the Church in African society. It is always surprising to Western observers to note the lack of depth in African Christianity, the superficiality of much that passes for the Christian religion. People are often Christian from other than spiritual motives. Christianity is not always accepted entirely on its own merits, but often because the old way of life has ceased to be satisfying and there is the hope that the Christian way may provide that sense of religious wholeness that the African needs. Religion is life, and Christianity will only survive in Africa if it can be experienced and enjoyed in living it out rather than in the formal intellectual choice to be a Christian. This kind of freedom of choice is rarely involved in Africa.

One of Africa's discoveries about the Christian faith is that it is concerned about the whole of life. The distinction between the religious and secular spheres that Western Christianity makes is new to the African. Africa is helping to restore a wholeness to Christianity. This involves a certain rebellion against the Western individualistic approach, but inevitably it often makes for superficial Christianity. This has to be reckoned with in making a judgment of African Christianity which appears to lack the energy of conviction to give it social and corporate purpose in African life. Is it to be a revolutionary leaven in African life, or only a conformity group that gradually succumbs to the drag and lethargy of African life?

He who seeks final answers in Africa is always in for surprises. The Christian Church must be both leavener and conformer in Africa, and in the vast changes in African life this is probably its finest role. As a leavener it has the immense task of purifying African life not in the manner of rigid negatives but in seeking to use tribal customs, traditions and manners that the glow of African life is continued within the Church. This job of leavening is a local, and often personal, witness on the part of Christians who are conscious of the anti-Christian tides sweeping round them in the form of secularism and of Islam. Both of those tides will eventually erode all that is finest and best in African life. Christianity's task is to preserve African life by leavening and purifying it.

For this reason Dr Spencer Trimingham in his survey *Islam in West Africa* says that he would prefer to see 'people superficially christianized rather than superficially islamized, since thereby barriers are broken down and they are open to deeper influences'. This means an open risk on the part of the Christian Church that it will 'conform' to certain practices, customs and habits which it knows to be at least doubtful, and sometimes definitely pagan. It could appear to be a mortal weakness for the Church, but it could be a strength for a developing Christianity to battle with these non-Christian elements within its life and eventually build them, purified and re-invigorated, into the wholeness of African Christian life.

The burden of African Christianity is that it is a child of unequal parentage—the West married to African life. It is still an adolescent dealing with an adolescent's problems of how to adjust and how to grow and be himself. If it were alone in the field its task of leavening and of avoiding too much conformity would be easier, but it has to meet the challenge of both secularism (also a child of the West) and of Islam at the same time. It is a warfare on two fronts, and out of the clash the form of a church which will not be fully identifiable with Western patterns will emerge. Indeed that is the rising hope for African Christianity as it both grows and glows round the Holy Table.

This brings us to an important point about the Christian faith which Africa may well reveal and emphasize. While we rightly stress the fact of the Church, and that no one can be a fully-orbed Christian without identification with it, yet the uniqueness of Christianity does not lie there. Nor does it lie in the Christian religion itself. It lies in the revelation of God in Christ. Too often the outward appearances of Christianity obscure this fact which they are meant to express, and thereby Christianity is disregarded and ignored. Too often it is not Christ who is lifted up by some caricature of him. The presence of Islam will always be for African Christianity a constant challenge to be clear and pertinent in its approach, remembering that the search for parallels between the two religions is not the final issue but the witness to the uniqueness of Christ.

Islam may well be a 'tutor unto Christ' for African Christianity by expecting from it a regular and insistent witness to his uniqueness. It is the presentation of Christ and his Gospel that will keep Africa in a state of perpetual discovery and will bring out new ideas and new ventures. This calls for charity always, a perpetual concern to understand, and an ability to think as the other man thinks. It must be admitted that not many ordinary Christians have these gifts especially when it comes to dealing with Islam, but the production of more of them will be one of Africa's discoveries and contributions to the wholeness of the faith.

In his book *The Call of the Minaret*, Kenneth Cragg, writing in the context of Christianity and Islam, sums up for Africa this sense of expectancy and discovery which is alive when the evangelistic element is Christ rather than the evangelists themselves:

> He who goes out humbly with Christ into the world of all races will perpetually discover the multiple, but constant, relevance of what he takes. Moreover, the transactions of such expression are mutual. It is the ruling conviction of the ecumenical movement within contemporary Christianity that it takes a whole world to understand a whole Christ. Those who take are not vulgarly universalizing their own culture: they are conveying that by the apprehensions of which both they and their hearts learn. If the claims of the Gospel are valid, it could not be otherwise (p. 183).

If it takes 'a whole world to understand a whole Christ', then it takes a whole Africa to understand what Christ means for the continent. I meditated on this point as I sat in the Third Assembly of the World Council of Churches at New Delhi and watched the procession of new African churches as their representatives took their places as members of the World Council. From Bantu churches at the Cape to Coptic churches in Cairo, Africa is now moving into the ecumenical movement with an eager vigour. As ease of movement and travel within Africa increases so the interchange of ideas and the creation of active fellowship will give African Christianity a total view of itself.

Already at the Mindolo Ecumenical Centre in Northern Rhodesia, Africa has a meeting place where the separated companies of Christ can assemble to see the continent as a whole. From tribalism to nationalism, and from nationalism to regionalism, and from regionalism to a continental conception of Africa: that is the natural progression of a Christian faith which can be satisfied with nothing less than a whole Africa for a whole Christ.

This is a discovery of our time, but the realization of it lies in the future. An ecumenical African Christianity had its first airing at the All Africa Conference at Ibadan in 1958, and there will be more such assemblies needed if this vision of the whole continent for Christ is to be sustained. That phrase sounds as if it were minted in a missionary society's office in London or New York in the mid-nineteenth century, but like many such phrases of that period it has the authentic Christian ring about it.

The establishment by the World Council of Churches of the Africa Church Conference with headquarters at Kitwe in the Copper Belt is a recognition of the need to take an 'Africa view' of Christianity. Under African leadership this Conference is to call the Africa Christian Education Conference at Salisbury in January 1963, to be followed by the Africa Church Assembly in Kampala in April 1963. Too many conferences, perhaps, and too much talk! But it is part of the present price to be paid in the growth of African Christianity.

Nothing less than a total Africa view will do justice to the Christian faith and to Africa as well. This continent was made for greatness, and it will be out of great Christian thinking and action that African Christianity will reveal the mystery and uniqueness of Christ to the African peoples.

8

RIM OF THE DAWN

I REMEMBER standing by Livingstone's statue at the Victoria Falls watching the rainbows flashing in the tumultuous spray of the Zambesi as the river leaped into the gorge. Light is everything in Africa, sharp, diamond crystal, and piercing in brilliance. It is never muted as in the soft sheen of English light. So it is with the dark. Anyone who has stood in the dark under a starlit African sky will know what I mean. This is the dark of darkness, deep and powerful.

But memorable as light and dark are in Africa, I think the rim of the dawn is the most memorable of all the shades of light the continent provides. Its purple, steel appearance on the horizon in a vast encompassing rim is there to see for only a few brief moments, for the value of an African dawn is not only in itself but in what follows it—the invigorating forenoon, the rising warmth of the sun, the heat of noon and the cool of the early evening. This rim of the dawn is the promise of power and achievement. It is not an inapt analogy of the position of the Christian faith and the Christian Church in Africa.

It can of course be shown that in some parts of Africa Christianity is long past the dawn, and is moving on towards noon. Some would say that a kind of cataclysmic night has descended on other parts of it, and there are vast areas where even the faint beginnings of the dawn are yet to appear. You can choose as you wish in Africa, and there will be always ample justification for your choice.

But it is the rim of the dawn for most of African Christianity. It is so in its Africanism, for the process of belonging to Africa is only just beginning as the Christian Church shakes itself free from its Western origins. It is so in the conception of the place of Christianity in the special and cultural life of Africa. How that is to be achieved, and what are the ways towards the achievement, are only just emerging into the discussions of the Christian Church. In its evangelistic thrust Christianity has yet to put forth its African strength and show that an indigenous Christianity can also be one which claims Africa not at the behest of Western missions but because evangelism is of the soul and strength of the African Church itself.

But if the dawn is only just breaking for Christianity in Africa there is much rich promise in the rim of light on the horizon, and the examples I offer in this chapter of the life of the Church could be multiplied by anyone who knows Africa. There as elsewhere the Christian Church is tested by its pastoral and personal presence. How does it minister, how does it comfort, how does it speak to the souls of men? After all the surveys, missions and commissions that Africa has endured (and must continue to endure) the Church is known for what it is in the local life of the people.

I had this point brought home to me very vividly one December morning as I walked in the sunshine outside the Bechuanaland town of Kanye. Ahead of me on the rough road was an open, flat-bottomed ox-wagon. It has no tented top as in the old days of southern African travel, but the span of twelve oxen were yoked to their task in the traditional manner. They had a heavy load. A dozen or more people squatted on the floor of the wagon, all dressed in dark, sombre clothes and looking very gloomy. In the middle of the wagon was a long wooden box, a coffin. It was a funeral procession, and even the oxen looked sad as they pulled at their yokes. Every few yards the wagon stopped, and one of the men got off to pick up a big stone to add to the ones already on the creaking wagon. It was evidently every mourner's duty to collect stones for the grave which was to be built out there in the bush where the jungle would creep over the burying place and envelop yet another nameless heap of stones in Africa.

At the head of the oxen walked an old African minister. He was wizened, grey and old, but his eyes were bright and his step lively. He waved a fly whisk as he walked and read aloud from the scriptures: 'The Lord has anointed me to bring good tidings to the afflicted; he has sent me to bind up the broken hearted . . . to comfort all that mourn.' The old man's voice rose and fell through the sunlit morning air. I could hear it above the scuffle of the oxen and the rumble of the wheels. The timeless rhythm of comfort which Christianity has carried round the world in so many tongues and conditions was being offered there on the dusty road.

I asked the old minister whether the people in the wagon belonged to the Church.

'No,' he said. 'They're not a Christian family. But their son has died. I'm giving him a Christian burial. I do it to give them some comfort.' The word *comfort* stuck in my memory. It is one of the marks of a mature Christian when he sees to the inner citadel of the Christian faith as one of comfort to the soul, and is then able to share his certainty with others. The old minister was turning what outwardly was a load of stones and a dead body into a chariot of triumph by his own serene faith which you could see shining in his face.

Christianity moves beyond the rim of the dawn in Africa when it consciously and in proper joy ministers to non-Christians, and regards them as within the parish of the pastor. Its peril is that of exclusiveness and separation. But the old minister at the head of the ox-waggon had got the clue which could lead to the breaking of many walls of partition in Africa which Christianity has allowed to grow up in areas where it is already well established. He had the unique gifts of comfort to offer at a decisive moment, and there he was in on the road displaying his gift in triumph.

It was in the same area of Africa that I met an example of Africa's own inner loyalty of spirit to its own institutions that Christianity must claim for itself if it is to be truly an African institution.

I was out with a missionary friend looking for the site of an old mission house which the years and the jungle had almost obliterated, but search as we would the site eluded us. We were about to give up the search when—as so often happens in Africa—out of the bush appeared a man. He led us straight to the spot.

The man carried a traveller's stick, and on his back was strapped his blanket with a bit of food inside it. His feet were bare and dusty. He looked tired for he had been on the trail all day long from the place where he had a large garden. The rains had beckoned him out to his land from the village. The corn must go in while the land was moist, and for days he had dug and planted. It was hard work and he had not finished.

What made him give up? As I asked him this question he stopped on the trail, as we walked together to the village, and looked me in the eyes. 'Master,' he said quite simply, 'the chief wants me.' That very morning he was digging his land when the news spread round that the chief—back home in the village—needed help on his own land. The man immediately stopped his own digging, packed his blanket, took his stick, and set off to obey the call of the chief.

In the simple phrase, 'the chief wants me', lies much of the true heart of Africa. It speaks for the Africa where personal relationships are paramount and intimate, and obedience is one of the first marks of loyalty. It speaks for the Africa where simple trust between man and man is the cement that holds life together. I met the chief. He is an educated man and a leading member of the church which, in this instance, is practically coterminous with the tribe. He thinks of himself as father of his people, and for them he represents the history and the tradition of the tribe, and is the centre piece of their community life. So when his call goes out through the bush, or through the villages, men drop their own business and tramp to the chief's house to answer his claim on their time and talents.

It all looks very feudalistic, and part of the old Africa which is rapidly eroding under the pressure of modern life. Democratic councils are replacing the direct rule of the chiefs, and where whole countries have leaped into independence a new set of relationships is imposed on the traditional African pattern. But personal loyalty and the cohesiveness of 'belonging' are in Africa's blood and will not be wholly eradicated by the new ways. The Church now has its chance of gearing the loyalties of the old Africa into its own life by showing that the church is the tribe which recognizes the 'chieftainship' of Jesus Christ. In him the desire to belong and the belief in community are fulfilled.

Africa could be the continent of community for the Christian faith, a land where the Church might recover her own, largely lost, sense of the *koinonia* of the believers in Christ. Africa sees religion as life itself. God is ever present in daily life, and it is daily life that a man has his links with his fellow men. The recovery of this understanding of what religion really is could be Africa's supreme gift to the Christian Church, and might well usher in a new age of faith.

But if Africa has the promise of this possibility for the Christian Church, the continent has already received from Christianity many gifts that foster this *koinonia* of believers. My examples are very simple ones but they go to the heart of what it is that turns inward assent to the faith into the actions of grace and character that betoken Christian maturity.

I was out in a remote area of the Bechuanaland Protectorate in the company of a missionary doctor. It was his dispensary day at a little post on the confines of the Kalahari country. As we lurched along in his truck he suddenly pointed ahead down the track, and shouted to me, 'There she is'.

I could see a woman standing in the roadway eagerly waving her hand to attract our attention. As we came nearer I could see that she held in one hand a piece of paper, and between the two fingers of the other hand there was something else. This turned out to be a sixpence. Her broad, brown face was covered with an immense grin. So was the doctor's.

It appeared that a month before the woman had come to the dispensary to see the doctor. She got a bottle of medicine. But she failed to produce the usual payment of sixpence. But the doctor trusted her on her simple promise to pay. That morning she tramped for ten miles through the bush to a spot on the road where the doctor would pass. She waited there for three hours with the bill, and the sixpence, a rendezvous of responsibility and resolution. 'I knew I could trust her,' remarked the doctor as he scribbled the receipt. 'It's not the sixpence that matters but the woman's attitude.'

I watched the woman return into the bush on her ten miles tramp homeward, proudly holding her piece of paper. She flashed a smile to us as she turned to wave.

Africa's response to Christianity may take many weird forms but the simplicities of the faith which emerge in personal conduct are also there to be counted on. They come out of the life of the Church, and are the products of long and patient nurture in preaching and in practice.

That same day I noted another example. The doctor brought me to his little thatched hut dispensary surrounded by a crowd of patients waiting to see him. It was a brilliant, blue morning, and the people were sitting about in the pleasant shade of the trees. It was a scene that is repeated a thousand times over across the face of Africa.

Under one of the trees I noticed a wheelbarrow. In it were a couple of very clean looking pillows. The wheelbarrow was a modern one with a rubber tyre on its front wheel, and the white pillows looked very comfortable. In fact it was all so inviting and the sun beginning to be so hot that I sat in the wheelbarrow myself just waiting in the true African manner for something to happen.

In due time the dispensary door opened and out came a woman limping very painfully, helped along by her husband. He led her gently towards the wheelbarrow. I got up and smoothed the pillows and held the wheelbarrow steady while he lifted her in. It was a tender, moving sight to see this tall gaunt African slowly lifting his sick wife into the wheelbarrow where she curled up in comfort on the pillows. Then proudly lifting the handles of the wheelbarrow he looked all round, at the doctor in the dispensary, at me and at the waiting crowd, and wheeled away his home-made ambulance into the bush.

'That's a miracle for you,' said the doctor as we watched them disappear. 'That's Africa. That man cares enough for his sick wife to wheel her in his barrow for twenty miles. He's been before. He'll come again and again until she's better.'

I noticed the doctor's emphasis on the word *cares*. In the old Africa that husband would not have cared enough about his wife to bring her all that way in his barrow. He might even have expected her to wheel him in the barrow! But the miracle of change in personal relationships has happened, and the growth of companionship between husband and wife is one of the fruits of the Christian spirit. African marriage can often mean for the woman only her fulfilment in child bearing and in the possession of children, and for the man someone to cook his food and provide his sexual pleasure. But married companionship is at the heart of Christian marriage, and I fancy the wheelbarrow husband and wife were practising it in the sunshine at the dispensary door and on the way home through the miles of bush. It is a mark of Christianity that is beyond the rim of the dawn, a sign of coming of age.

But is the private character of the African Christian reflected in public affairs? It is in the realm of politics and social relationships that African Christianity is having to stand up to the test. Are the virtues of grace, tolerance and forbearance which appear in the private character of so many African Christians also seen in the public affairs of the continent?

The most obvious testing point is in race relationships, and there is ample evidence for and against the growth of Christanity in this area of public conduct. I cannot here attempt to assess the movement of opinion towards the betterment of race relations in Africa which are expertly analysed by such organizations as the Institute of Race Relations in Johannesburg. Nor would it be just to claim that any betterment in areas like South Africa and Southern Rhodesia is directly the result of the life and activity of the Christian Church. Many other factors enter into the making of a pattern of humane race relationships in Africa, even the derided *apartheid doctrine* itself having the reverse effect that its prophets expect. The emphasis of *apartheid* on separation has raised the issue of co-operation and integration between the races. It has elevated the Christian teaching of no discrimination so sharply that all Africa, and indeed all the world, is aware of what is at stake.

My example of a new atmosphere in race relations comes from the world of sport, and therefore may not be directly attributed to the influence of Christianity except that it would be possible to claim that the steady appreciation of what is the Christian thing to do (without mentioning the word 'Christian') is the result of much Christian witness in this vexed field of public concern.

It was a December afternoon in 1958. 4,000 people had gathered on the university athletic ground in Salisbury, Southern Rhodesia, to see a race between Gordon Pirie, the Olympic champion, and Yotham Muleya, a nineteen-year-old motor mechanic from Northern Rhodesia. Muleya, a star runner in his own small world, had never pitted himself in a race like this before, and many people wondered how long he would last against Pirie.

For weeks before the race the athletic authorities of Salisbury had been against Muleya running. No black man had ever run against a white man in Rhodesia. It was argued that this was an all-white athletic meeting and the decision was taken against Muleya running. Rhodesian sportsmen were troubled, and so was Pirie who let it be known that he could not take part in a segregated meeting. Eventually the steady pressure of public opinion compelled the committee to change its view.

The young African lined up with the white champion, a forlorn opponent to Pirie who pounded round the first lap at tremendous speed. Muleya hung on to him through the second, third, fourth and fifth laps. In the sixth, Pirie glanced anxiously over his shoulder, Muleya was still there and running splendidly. Pirie could not throw him off. Then came the eighth lap, and in it Muleya shot ahead, and to the crowd's amazement streaked in front of Pirie at the tape by two hundred yards.

How the crowd cheered! I can still hear the sound of that mighty roar. They rose to the African runner as one man, and in that moment colour, prejudice, tradition and discrimination all disappeared in the celebration of a fine victory. One old Southern Rhodesian commented as he left the ground, 'Times have changed. We must accept the African in the world of sport'.

I am not claiming this as a victory for the Church of Christ but as one of those indirect victories which Christianity must expect to see as Africa moves along to the road of more general acceptance of Christian values in public conduct. These are amongst the events that help to make a Christian nation.

In thinking of Africa and the kind of Christianity and Christian Church that she will produce as her day moves on towards high noon, one is continually compelled to meditate on the personal event that one remembers rather than to record the big programme of achievements. African Christianity combined with Western aid is not without her calendar of red-letter events such as the united Christian front offered to the Copper Belt, the range of Christian community centres at Nairobi, the Wilgespruit venture of race relations near Johannesburg, the all-Africa radio plan 'Voice of the Gospel' from Addis Ababa, the various schemes for united action in theological education, in serving leprosy sufferers, and in the care of the blind and the handicapped.

But the heart of compassion in Africa was opened to me one morning outside the great Muslim city of Zaria where in Wusasa the Christians have lived for years in the shadow of Islam. I noticed a man walking towards me down the village street. He was barefooted and dressed in a long robe. He came slowly along, feeling his way by tapping with his stick. He was blind.

We sat down by the roadside to talk. He was the village postman, messenger and general errand man. He had heard that a stranger had arrived in the village so he came along to greet me. He had two parcels with him. Out of one came a typewriter and there on the roadside he tapped out on a piece of rough paper a message in the Braille language: a message of welcome to me and a greeting to friends in England.

Then he unwrapped his second parcel. Out came a large book about the size of a family Bible. Made of thick brown paper, the pages were studded with Braille characters. He ran his fingers along the lines until he found the passage from St John 14: 'Let not your heart be troubled; believe in God, believe also in me.'

We sat there by the side of the dusty road in silence. Then he packed his treasures, shook hands, and away he padded down the road. I watched him tapping, tapping with his stick, feeling his way along. A blind man in Africa, and such a happy one! I was moved by the man's inner serenity. He had turned blindness into sight, and dark into light, not only for himself but for the whole company of the *koinonia* in that place, and for me, the stranger, too. Handicapped since boyhood, he had with the help of a Christian fellowship turned his handicap into a triumph, a living witness to what care and the proper teaching can do.

Christianity has brought many gifts to Africa, education, respect for children and women, and has provided for the traditional African society values which have disrupted and enriched it. In the hundred years or so of its modern attempt to occupy the continent Christianity has offered to Africa no greater gift than that of compassion. The blind man of Wusasa was evidence of it and anyone with a little knowledge of the continent will be able to add examples of this divine offering without which Christianity often becomes a poor and thin spectacle, possessing the teaching but omitting the practice. It was compassion that compelled the army of confessors to serve Africa during the last hundred years. It is compassion of the deep and eternal kind which Christ displayed on the Cross that will eventually win Africa for him.

The engrossing question for the Christian faith in Africa is whether the roots of compassion, confession and consecration are laid deep enough now in Africa's life, or whether the withering storms that have in the past blasted her Christianity will prevail again. I do not know the answer.

But I have asked the question of myself, in hope, as I have watched the expectant richness of African life in the host of young men and women gathered for worship in the chapels of the universities at Ibadan, Makerere and Accra. I also asked the same question as I sat in the tiny mud and thatch church of a group of the Birom people on the Nigerian plateau amidst their pastoral corn stockades, and amongst a group of Tonga people down in the heat haze of the Zambesi valley. It is the prime question for Christians in the Copper Belt, in the lands of *apartheid*, as well as in the countries where black freedom marches on.

I claim no more for Christianity in Africa than the rim of the dawn. But having claimed that, I must in Christian hope expect the forenoon, and some day the high noon itself.

POSTSCRIPT

IT IS always dangerous to prophesy about Africa as the continent, in spite of its obvious handicaps, is capable of producing something quite new in politics, citizenship, in government and in the Church. This possibility continues to hold a fascination for the observer in all these fields of African life, and they are even more fascinating now that Africa has thrown off so much of the tutelage which the colonial powers once provided.

Politically African countries will be 'strong' in the sense that they will run to 'one party' states centred round a 'personality' who will accumulate authority into his own hands. This is an alarming prospect for traditional western democrats who see so many of their political theories being dismissed out of hand by those they think of as 'inexperienced' in the ways of government.

There will be many more surprises to come as Africa moves into her stride, and those countries of the West who give material aid will not be exempt from brusque treatment.

Two areas where the shape of things to come will have decisive effects on the future of the continent are the Republic of South Africa and the countries of Central Africa which have been uneasily grouped together as the Central Africa Federation. In South Africa the long night of *apartheid* moves on towards the dawn, for the Afrikaner people, of 'separate nations' in which the Bantu will be forcibly held within their own 'homelands'. For other South Africans, and most people outside South Africa, it is a movement deeper into the night of final misery and destruction as the tragedy is played out in the sunshine and material prosperity of South Africa.

There are those who believe that now the Republic is in existence and has moved out of the Commonwealth, and Afrikaner pride has duly triumphed, the Afrikaner will look again at the precarious position at the southern tip of the continent, and see the hopelessness of his 'container' policy. It may be that there are sufficient reserves of political, economic and Christian sense in the Republic of South Africa to lay the foundations of a multi-racial nation. But it would be unwise to expect this while the power to enforce the present 'solution' is in the hands of the white minority, and while the bulk of the Christian Church in South Africa acquiesces in it.

It must be admitted that many sincere hopes and dreams of non-racial Central Africa Federation have been drowned in the Zambesi. What began ten years ago as a genuine attempt at 'partnership' between the races has failed through distrust, and lack of confidence, and for this failure the white man must bear the main responsibility. It is true that time and the swift movements of the African revolution have overtaken the Central African plan. Unfortunately, it was from the beginning a 'white man's plan' and never won the confidence of the people of African race, and its passing is a warning that whatever economic, or other, association there may be in the future between the Rhodesias and Nyasaland, it must from the start have the confidence of all the people.

If the numbers of Christians, as given in this book, are any guide to Africa's Christian future then there ought to be a mighty Church in Africa. With a Christian community far bigger than in India or China, African Christianity has the immense task of helping to create a Christian continent. In many ways it has to create life out of a vacuum, and to fashion an African society which is poised between an allegiance to what is traditionally African and 'the things' that are eagerly sought for in the modern world. Christianity has to provide values and judgments for Africa which arise out of what is eternal, and to help Africa to see that 'the things' she desires are not after all the foundation of life.

Alas, how often the white man in Africa appears to have an unshakable belief in 'the things', and from him Africa has learned all too easily that 'the things' do go a long way in providing the 'good life'. To balance this view the Christian Church has to offer a Gospel which is both communal and personal, a Gospel of 'things' as well as 'spirit', and the African response will not always be in the manner that western Christianity understands or respects. To measure African Christianity by the yardstick of nineteenth-century individualism in religion, as known in Europe and North America, will always lead to misguided conclusions.

For this divine task the Church in Africa needs leaders of peculiar insight and sensitivity who will not take all their cues from the West, but be capable of fashioning an African character for Christianity. We are not likely to see this accomplishment in the generation that must still have its Christian roots in 'mission' and 'missionary' and what they did in the days of their ascendancy. Africa's memory and devotion to the past are long and deep, and the Church will be a long time moving out of its 'mission' cocoon. I never forget the spontaneous hug I was given by a very old African woman who thought I resembled a missionary she once knew, and he had been dead at least fifty years!

As for missions themselves, there must still be a place for them under the control of the African Church who will no doubt want them in the staffing and management of the Church. But to use the expressive phrase of John Taylor, Africa Secretary of the Church Missionary Society, 'missions must sink into the landscape'.[1]

[1] Mr Taylor has written four important surveys: *Christianity and Politics in Africa* (Pelican Books), *The Growth of the Church in Buganda, Christians of the Copperbelt* (with D. Lehmann) and *The Primal Vision: Christian Presence Amid African Religion* (all SCM Press).

All this lends high importance to the plans for lifting the standards of the Christian ministry in Africa, the equipping of theological seminaries, and the provision of literature and libraries. It also demands Church unity in the training of the ministry even before there can be organic union of the churches.

'Oh to be in Africa now that independence is there!' It was a satirical cry I once heard from the lips of one who had given a lifetime's devoted work in Africa. He had had some hard knocks, and for those who work in and for Africa there are many more to come. Africa is a continent that draws and devours her lovers, and some turn sour and cynical at the continent's antics. But the Christian man must go on both serving and believing in Africa.

SUGGESTIONS FOR READING

A Short History of Africa by Roland Oliver and J. D. Fage (Penguin), an excellent survey of Africa from pre-recorded history times to the present with a nice lot of maps. In the same series *African Profiles* by Ronald Segal deals with some of the famous people in Africa. Then there is *Introducing Christianity* by E. H. Pyle and S. G. Williamson (Penguin) done by two men who 'taught' Christianity in Ghana. What they wisely say is applicable everywhere.

The Planting of Christianity in Africa (four volumes, Lutterworth) by C. P. Groves is a comprehensive survey of how Christianity came to Africa and how it has fared up to 1954.

In the World's Classics series (Oxford Press) *South African Explorers* and *East African Explorers* provide a most readable flavour of the mixed bag of people who have tramped about Africa—all in their own words.

INDEX